The Ethical Leadership Scales

Ethical Competence Scale
Ethical Leadership Scale
Ethical Organization Scale

3 Tools to Develop and Measure Ethical Competence in Individuals, Leaders and Organizations

with supporting essays calling for a post-modern perspective on Ethical Leadership as the gold standard in human relationships

Desmond Berghofer PhD
Geraldine Schwartz PhD

www.trafford.com

North America & international
toll-free: 844-688-6899 (USA & Canada)
fax: 812 355 4082

Contents

Acknowledgements

As the authors of these Scales we have read widely in the fields of ethics, leadership, emotional intelligence and positive psychology over the last two decades. While it would be impossible to list all of our sources, it is important to acknowledge that the development of the scales comes from wide reading in these fields.

We would in particular like to acknowledge the contribution to our thinking and to the creation of the Ethical Leadership Scales of several outstanding authors, leaders and teachers: Peter Kostenbaum, Peter Senge, Stephen Covey, Daniel Goleman, Martin Selligman, Robert Greenleaf, Margaret Wheatley, Patricia Aburdene, James Kouzes and Barry Posner. The pioneering work of these authors and their continuing influence contributes to the foundations of the new discipline of Ethical Leadership.

With regard to technical support, we especially acknowledge Pat Dobie whose skill in formatting the content of the Scales and good-humored patience throughout made the task of creating this book much less onerous than it would otherwise have been.

Finally, we would like to acknowledge the influence and support of our many colleagues and students whose comments and questions over the years have helped us immeasurably in developing the ideas presented in the Scales in Part 1 and in the essays in Parts 2 and 3.

Desmond Berghofer PhD
Geraldine Schwartz PhD

January 2008

Prologue

*Ethical Leadership speaks in a new voice for all humanity
as the 21ˢᵗ century moves through its first decade.*

The central values for the good life in a global civilization are relationships of trust and respect anchored in integrity. In this declaration the sacred and secular enter common cause across all human divisions and boundaries. Successful enterprise of any size depends on such relationships between individuals, communities, organizations and countries. Moreover, in our time, when the very planet that sustains life is under siege, such relationships must extend beyond the human world to include the whole of the biosphere. Citizens, organizations and governments everywhere are called to recognize their intimate connection to life giving systems of air, water and earth that we all share.

If the generations now in charge promote these self-evident truths as the central value of our time, we will leave a legacy of great worth to the generations who follow us. If we fail to establish such relationships at all levels of interaction, the evidence is already clear that future prospects on Earth will be greatly diminished.

This book is about these large and profound issues of common cause. The Ethical Leadership Scales and the dialogue they engender are the tools and process that can help to enhance the skills of ethical leadership needed to take us forward into a safe and secure future. The essays that follow in Part 2 provide further substance for consideration of what it means to be an ethical leader at every level. In Part 3 the ideas are extended to the global village, reflecting the values contained in the section on global issues found in the Ethical Leadership Scales.

We live in "the best of times" when human knowledge has created institutions that are the apex of collective wisdom about how we should live and care for each other and the Earth. We also live in "the worst of times" when the dark side of humanity reflected in violence, war, greed, corruption, dishonesty and malfeasance of every kind is also at its apex. We have the opportunity now to choose for the best or the worst, for a future pregnant with possibility or one in which none of us would want to live. The principles embedded in ethical leadership provide the filter to help us embrace the choice for good.

Introduction

With these Scales you have in your hands the means to develop and measure your competence in ethical behavior. Acting ethically requires personal qualities and a set of skills that enable you to form relationships with others built on trust and service. We develop these qualities and skills through experience and through commitment to be ethical in our dealings with other people. The extent to which we develop the necessary qualities and skills is a measure of our ethical competence. The Ethical Leadership Scales provide a comprehensive and rigorous way to think about and judge the extent to which you have developed your ethical competence. More importantly, when used in a learning situation they enable each of us to improve, to become more ethical in our daily interactions in business and personal life.

Why is this important?

Being ethical is the gold standard for success in life. Ethical relationships are built into the fabric of the universe. It operates on universal laws, such as "do no harm" and "treat others with respect." When honored these universal laws ensure good outcome. It may not always be the outcome we expect or even desire, but we can be sure that it is the right outcome in the circumstances. If we act in contradiction to these universal laws, we can be certain that no long term good will come of it, even if the immediate results seem to be beneficial. The universe operates on principles of cooperation, mutual support and reciprocity. It returns to us what we give. If we build our human relationships with each other and with the natural world on these laws, we will know the joy of success. Conversely, if we act in contradiction to these universal principles, we will experience the consequences in many and varied ways that eventually lead to distress and possibly breakdown. That is why knowing what the ethical principles or laws are, and acting in accordance with them, is so important. The Ethical Leadership Scales are meant to assist with this knowledge and practice.

There are also biological reasons for honoring ethical principles. Modern biology and positive psychology reveal through an extensive body of research that the internal chemistry that supports our life and well-being is being driven and molded to a very large extent, and for better or for worse, by others. If the relationships in which we find ourselves are characterized by unethical behavior, we pay the cost in stress and even illness. While we cannot necessarily control the behavior of others, we can ensure that our own actions are not contributing to this problem, and we can be a model for right action to others.

What are the fundamental ethical principles?

The ethical principles that govern all of life are known through the wisdom traditions that have come down to us over the ages. They are now being confirmed by modern science as we gain deeper understanding about the fundamental nature of reality. Foremost among these principles are *trust, respect, integrity, honesty, fairness, equity, justice* and *compassion*. One of the most ancient understandings we have that embodies the essence of these principles is the Golden Rule, which emerged in several different spiritual traditions in the ancient world some 2500 years ago in a time known as the Axial Age. It is stated in different ways in the different traditions, but we most commonly know it as: "Do unto others as you would have them do unto you."

The wisdom of the Golden Rule was given deeper meaning by the German philosopher, Immanuel Kant, in the eighteenth century when he declared that in any relationship it is important to always treat the other person as an *end* and never merely as a *means* to serve your own personal interests. Another German philosopher and theologian, Martin Buber, described successful ethical relationships as *"I-Thou"* relationships in which people recognize the intrinsic worth of others and always treat them with sincerity and respect. The Ethical Leadership Scales are designed to elicit these fundamental ethical understandings and allow you to reflect on the extent to which you are honoring them in your personal and business life. The Scales provide a platform on which your own ethical responses may be honed and developed, thus increasing your competence and consequently your well-being and enjoyment of life.

Organization of this book

This book is organized in three parts. Part 1, called The Scales, contains three Scales which together comprise the Ethical Leadership Scales. These are meant to be completed by you the reader under direction from a teacher or facilitator trained in their use and administration. The first Scale is called the "Ethical Competence Scale" and is designed to enable the user to reflect privately on his or her own level of competence with regard to each of the 30 items on the Scale.

The second Scale is the "Ethical Leadership Scale," which contains 40 items relating to the qualities and skills of an ethical leader. It is designed for the user to reflect on his or her own qualities as a leader who models ethical behavior and who encourages others to act ethically in everything they do. This Scale may also be completed as an assessment of the ethical leadership skills of another person who is a designated leader in an organization or in the community. When used in this way the intent is for people in the team or unit under the direction of this leader to provide feedback on his or her leadership skills. Again, this Scale should be used under the direction of a teacher or facilitator trained in its use.

The third Scale is the "Ethical Organization Scale." This Scale is intended for use by the leadership team of an organization to assess the ethical behavior of the organization with respect to 10 items covering internal and external relationships. Under the direction of a teacher or facilitator trained in its use this Scale provides a means for the leadership team to reflect at first privately and then collectively on how well their organization is doing as an ethical leader in its field. Because leaders come from different parts of the organization, they will bring different perspectives to the discussion, which can provide fertile ground for problem solving and creative thinking about what might need to be done to improve things.

Part 2 of the book is called "Perspectives on Ethical Leadership." It contains a few short essays on different aspects of ethical leadership, which we have prepared from several years of reflection and discussion through the work of the Institute for Ethical Leadership. We founded the Institute in Vancouver, Canada in 1998 to provide a vehicle for leaders to come together to consider issues of ethical leadership in various theme areas such as Stewardship and the Environment, Health and Wellness, Youth and Education, Business and Sustainability, and Relationships and Personal Development. More information about the Institute and its work can be found at the website www.ethicalleadership.com. All of the essays in Part 2 complement the content of the Scales in Part 1 and as a reader you are encouraged to use them to extend your knowledge and sensitivity to the importance of ethical behavior to our society.

In Part 3, "Global Ethical Perspectives," the discussion is widened to show how the kind of knowledge we create determines the kind of world we build, and how the application of the feminine perspective can move that world towards the ideal of peace and security that lies at the heart of human longing.

How are the Scales meant to be used?

The essential purpose of the Ethical Leadership Scales is to develop ethical competence and to enhance the skills of ethical leadership. While some benefit is provided to anyone who reads the Scales, they are not intended for casual reading, but rather to be used in a teaching/learning situation under the direction of a teacher or facilitator trained in their use. The three elements of the learning process in play with the use of the Scales are *personal reflection, dialogue* and *feedback*.

Quiet personal reflection is absolutely essential when one is considering issues of ethical behavior. How we think and act in relation to others derives from a deep part of our personal consciousness. Here the teaching we have received from parents, mentors and others who have influenced us, beginning at a very early age, along with the lessons we have learned from life, come together in our own personal mindstate. The Scales are intended to help you examine your mindstate with respect to your relationships towards others and to form judgments about your level of ethical competence in regard to these relationships.

Following personal reflection, dialogue with others about the meaning of what you have been considering is another essential part of ethical learning. It is through dialogue that we are exposed to different perspectives and come to a deeper understanding about our own beliefs and actions. If full benefit is to be derived from the use of the Scales, it is important that you have the opportunity for dialogue with others, who have also completed the Scale, under the direction of a trained teacher or facilitator.

By completing the Scale and discussing it with others you are receiving vital feedback, which is the third element of the learning process incorporated in the design of the Scales. All of us learn best when we have a sense of how well we are doing in regard to some form of a measure. By incorporating a quantitative measure (discussed more fully below) the Scales encourage you to think in terms of how well you are doing at the moment and how you might improve. A section that asks you to specifically identify your strengths and areas for improvement creates the opportunity for you to benefit from feedback to yourself. When this is shared and discussed with others (under proper direction) the feedback effect is greatly enhanced.

The quantitative measure used in the Scales is the Ethical Quotient.

What is the Ethical Quotient?

The well understood measure for intellectual (cognitive) intelligence is the Intelligence Quotient, commonly known as IQ. We have used the same concept of a quotient in measuring competence on each of the three scales presented here. The total score is calculated out of 100 and called a quotient, with 100 being the highest or most ideal measure. The scales with their respective quotients are as follows:

> The Ethical Competence Scale leading to the Ethical Quotient (EthQ)
> The Ethical Leadership Scale leading to the Ethical Leadership Quotient (EthLQ)
> The Ethical Organization Scale leading to the Ethical Organization Quotient (EthOQ)

Using this framework you can calculate the respective quotient for each Scale by following the method for scoring.

What is the method for scoring each Scale?

In completing a Scale you are making a series of personal judgments on individual items in the Scale. The Ethical Competence Scale has 30 items; the Ethical Leadership Scale has 40 items; and the Ethical Organization Scale has 10 items. Each item is accompanied by a set of bullets to give a clear understanding of what the item means. You are asked to consider each item and its set of explanations carefully. Based on your current thinking and current actions and behaviors, you are asked to assign a value or score for that item.

The judgment is made according to the following key:

> If you believe the quality or characteristic is **always in place** give it 10 or 9.
> If you believe the quality or characteristic is **usually in place** give it 8 or 7.
> If you believe the quality or characteristic is **sometimes in place** give it 6 or 5.
> If you believe the quality or characteristic is **rarely in place** give it 4 or 3.
> If you believe the quality or characteristic is **never in place** give it 2 or 1.

To arrive at the exact score for each item, proceed in this way. Choose the value category that on first consideration seems most appropriate. For example, if you think the quality or characteristic is **usually in place**, you will be considering a score of 8 or 7. Now read each explanation carefully. If you think that one of the explanations suggests a weakness, give the item the lower score of 7. If you think two of the explanations suggest weakness, go down to the next category of **sometimes in place** and assign a score of 6. If more than two of the explanations suggest weakness, you will need to consider an even lower score. Place the final score for each item in its respective column.

When you have completed all of the items, add the values to get a total score. You will then need to divide that score by the number indicated on each scale to get a Quotient. **For convenient reference copy all of the values onto the Personal Record Form**. As a final step record in the space provided (the Scale Profile) the items which you consider to be your top three strengths and the items you consider to be most in need of development. You can also record in the space provided on this profile any personal thoughts or comments you have after completing the Scale.

Completing any of the Scales in this way provides you with a quotient and a profile for the particular day on which you completed the Scale. This is the *personal reflection* component of the learning process. Under the direction of the teacher or facilitator you will then use this content as the basis for *dialogue* with others about the process and what it means in that particular situation. This provides the *feedback* component of the learning process.

It is important to emphasize that each Scale is meant to be used as a personal private instrument for individual reflection. Personal honesty in completing each Scale is essential in order to achieve the maximum benefit.

The Scales can also be used for research in order to provide further information on the group under consideration, or to evaluate the use of a particular intervention meant to enhance ethical leadership.

How are the Scales used for research?

The Ethical Leadership Scales may be used as part of an applied research intervention to measure changes in ethical competence based on this intervention. As this is a specific use of the Scales requiring a detailed explanation, the full description of how to use the Scales in a research situation is provided in the Appendix. Please consult the Appendix if you are interested in using the Scales for research purposes.

Final words

The Ethical Leadership Scales contained in Part 1 complemented by the essays on ethical leadership in Part 2 and by the essays on the global perspective in Part 3, provide a rigorous and comprehensive approach to the teaching and learning of ethical leadership. In preparing this material our purpose was to put into the hands of interested and concerned citizens a means to enhance the quality of ethical behavior across all sectors of local and global society. We have emphasized that the Scales should be administered by facilitators trained in their use, and to that end we have designed training programs for Facilitators of Ethical Leadership. For further information about the nature and scope of this initiative on Ethical Leadership in its broadest application, and to contact the authors, please consult the website www.ethicalleadership.com. We believe that study and dialogue on how to raise ethical standards in relationships of all kinds are among the most important initiatives for humanity at this critical stage of our social and moral evolution. We wish all who are engaged in that work every possible success and we stand ready to assist in any way we can.

PART 1

The Scales

Ethical Competence Scale

Ethical Competence Scale

Introduction

The Ethical Competence Scale is made up of 30 items divided into three sectors:
1.   Personal Ethical Competence: How we maintain our personal commitment to an ethical life – numbers 1-12
2.   Social Ethical Competence: How we handle relationships – numbers 13-24
3.   Global Ethical Competence: How we see the Earth and all life on it as a web of delicate connections requiring stewardship for sustainability – numbers 25-30

The Personal Ethical Competence sector is subdivided into subsections:
1.   Foundational Characteristics
       - How we are guided in thought and action
       - numbers 1-7
2.   Action Characteristics
       - How we act in support of our foundational beliefs and values
       - numbers 8-12

The Social Ethical Competence sector is divided into two subsections:
1.   Empathy
       - How we strive to understand and appreciate the worth of others
       - numbers 13-17
2.   Social Skills
       - How we act to induce desirable, ethically grounded responses in others
       - numbers 18-24

The Global Ethical Competence sector is divided into two subsections:
1.   Connections
       - How we act as part of a complex interconnected whole
       - numbers 25-27
2.   Future Orientation
       - How we act as responsible participants in creating a mutually beneficial future
       - numbers 28-30

Together, the 30 items on this scale provide a thorough, representative description of an individual's mindstate (consciousness) and characteristic actions (behavior). It is a measure that reflects the current state of a person's ethical competence at the time the test is taken.

How to Use the Scale

To complete the Ethical Competence Scale read the introduction and following comments carefully, so that you understand the purpose, assumptions and construction of the scale.

Consider each item and its explanations thoughtfully. Base your score value category selection on an honest perusal of your current thoughts and actions. Remember that this information is for your personal use only.

Once you have selected a score value category, review the various ways in which this characteristic is described. If one of the aspects is weaker than the others, choose the lower of the two numbers in that score value category. If two items are weaker, choose the higher number in the score value category below. If more than two are weaker, choose the score value category below your first choice.

For example: 'Trustworthiness'. You have chosen *'usually in place' (8 or 7)*. However, you can think of instances where you have been unwilling to admit your mistakes. You would then choose the lower number *(7)* for the value. As you consider further, you can remember several instances where you have not kept your promises. You would then go to the higher number of the score value category below, *('sometimes in place')*. You would then have a value of *6*. If after further consideration you think that any other of the explanations are not usually the way you act or feel, you may want to reconsider the category you chose first and answer, *'sometimes in place' (6-5)*.

After you have considered each of the 30 items separately and have recorded a value for each, add up your score out of 300 and divide by three to get the EthQ. Record this number in the correct space. Then consider your personal strengths and areas for improvement and record them in the space provided. Finally, copy all of your scores onto the Personal Record Form for quick reference at a later time.

Remember, this Quotient is a reflection of your thinking at this time. It is not a fixed value. Doing this test should make you more aware of your characteristic mindstate and actions. This is the beginning of all change and growth. Or, you may be very satisfied with your current mindstate and doing this test will serve to affirm your thought and action.

Use the following Score Values to record the nature of your thinking and actions at this time.

This characteristic is:			
Always in place	10-9	Rarely in place	4-3
Usually in place	8-7	Never in place	2-1
Sometimes in place	6-5		

Ethical Competence Scale
Personal Ethical Competence
How we maintain our personal commitment to an ethical life

Foundational Characteristics	How we are grounded in thought and action	Always in Place: 10-9 Usually in Place: 8-7 Sometimes in Place: 6-5 Rarely in Place: 4-3 Never in Place: 2-1				
Characteristic	Explanation	10 -9	8- 7	6- 5	4- 3	2- 1
1.Trustworthiness	• Being reliable and dependable • Being willing to admit mistakes • Being true to your word • Being worthy of confidence • Keeping promises					
2. Conscientious-ness	• Taking responsibility for personal performance • Meeting commitments on time to the best of your ability • Being thorough • Being accountable • Being careful in ethical matters • Considering the matter from others' perspectives					
3. Consistency	• Maintaining a consistent level of dependability • Maintaining a consistent level of ethical behavior • Avoiding contradictory behavior • Being consistent in your work life and personal life					
4. Steadfastness	• Being constant and unchanging in accountability • Being there for others • Sticking to your guns where you feel you are right					
5. Integrity	• Being completely sincere • Being decent and fair • Being honest • Being truthful, not false • Keeping your word					
6. Transparency	• Being open and truthful • Avoiding secretive behavior • Not keeping hidden agendas					

Personal Ethical Competence Cont'd.

Action Characteristics	How we act in support of our foundational beliefs and values	Always in Place: 10-9 Usually in Place: 8-7 Sometimes in Place: 6-5 Rarely in Place: 4-3 Never in Place: 2-1				
Characteristic	Explanation	10-9	8-7	6-5	4-3	2-1
7. Learning Oriented	• Showing a commitment and eagerness for new learning • Being willing to embrace new knowledge • Being open to new understanding that may impact ethical standards • Being willing to commit time, effort and resources to new learning					
8. Courage	• Showing willingness to risk and persevere in support of standards and principles • Being willing to stand alone, even when others disagree • Being willing to stand up in face of opposition and criticism • Being willing to act for right cause even in the face of fear or personal pain					
9. Determination	• Showing willingness to persevere to achieve worthy objectives • Willing to work long and hard for right outcome • Showing strength in persisting to accomplish what you set out to do					
10. Optimism	• Maintaining hope and enthusiasm • Operating from belief in ultimate success to achieve the good outcome • Looking for the bright side, for the positive aspects					
11. Initiative	• Being ready to seize opportunities to promote worthy outcomes • Showing enterprise in pursuing ethical objectives • Being creative and entrepreneurial in outlook					
12. Thorough-ness	• Covering the waterfront • Paying attention to details to ensure nothing is overlooked that could adversely affect the right outcome • Considering all possible aspects to promote the greater good					

Social Ethical Competence
How we handle relationships

Empathy	How we strive to understand and appreciate the worth of others	Always in Place: 10-9 Usually in Place: 8-7 Sometimes in Place: 6-5 Rarely in Place: 4-3 Never in Place: 2-1				
Characteristic	Explanation	10-9	8-7	6-5	4-3	2-1
13. Understanding Others	• Being sensitive to others' feelings and perspectives • Taking an active interest in others' concerns • Being attentive to emotional cues • Listening deeply • Being willing to change our mind or direction to accommodate others as long as the ethical foundation remains secure • Being able to walk in someone else's shoes					
14. Respecting Others	• Showing respect and consideration for others regardless of ethnicity, age, gender or occupation • Respecting the disadvantaged, the handicapped and the poor • Treating all people with dignity • Showing respect for the rights of others • Seeking to understand diverse world views • Seeing diversity as an opportunity to create a richer social environment					
15. Caring about Others	• Showing genuine care and concern for the well-being of others • Acting with compassion • Showing concern for others at all times • Treating others fairly • Rewarding and honoring others without discrimination					

Social Ethical Competence Cont'd.

Empathy	How we strive to understand and appreciate the worth of others	Always in Place: 10-9 Usually in Place: 8-7 Sometimes in Place: 6-5 Rarely in Place: 4-3 Never in Place: 2-1				
Characteristic	Explanation	10-9	8-7	6-5	4-3	2-1
16. Developing Others	• Acknowledging and rewarding ethical behavior in others • Offering useful feedback • Identifying people's needs for further ethical growth • Mentoring, giving timely coaching • Challenging others to grow and change in positive ways • Supporting others in their attempts to grow even when they make mistakes					
17. Serving Others	• Anticipating, recognizing and meeting the needs of others • Being committed to delivering the highest possible service to others • Being mindful of the need to serve all who serve you • Matching your services to the needs of others • Seeking ways to increase satisfaction for those you serve • Gladly offering appropriate assistance • Acting as a trusted advisor					

Social Ethical Competence Cont'd.

Social Skills	How we act to induce desirable, ethically grounded responses in others	Always in Place: 10-9 Usually in Place: 8-7 Sometimes in Place: 6-5 Rarely in Place: 4-3 Never in Place: 2-1				
Characteristic	Explanation	10-9	8-7	6-5	4-3	2-1
18. Communication	• Sending clear, transparent messages, avoiding mixed messages • Seeking to be clearly understood • Participating effectively in give-and-take • Dealing with difficult issues straightforwardly • Welcoming full sharing of information • Staying receptive to bad news as well as good • Making it a point to keep others informed					
19. Conflict Management	• Handling difficult people and tense situations with diplomacy and tact • Anticipating potential conflict • Bringing disagreements into the open and helping to de-escalate • Encouraging debate and open discussion • Orchestrating win-win solutions • Listening for the other person's point of view • Searching for common ground					
20. Inspiration	• Raising enthusiasm for accepting and accomplishing ethical, worthwhile challenges • Arousing enthusiasm for a shared worthy vision • Inspiring others to feel good about what you are asking or doing					
21. Building Bonds	• Seeking out and nurturing relationships that are mutually beneficial • Cultivating and maintaining informal networks • Building rapport and keeping others in the loop • Making and maintaining personal friendships with an ethical base • Being a good friend					

Social Ethical Competence Cont'd.

Social Skills	How we act to induce desirable, ethically grounded responses in others	Always in Place: 10-9 Usually in Place: 8-7 Sometimes in Place: 6-5 Rarely in Place: 4-3 Never in Place: 2-1				
Characteristic	Explanation	10-9	8-7	6-5	4-3	2-1
22. Cooperation	• Being willing to work together with others on a shared vision or goal • Looking for ways to work together • Being willing to partner other people's projects					
23. Collaboration	• Actively working with others toward shared goals • Sharing plans, information and resources • Valuing shared work and experiences • Putting effort into ways of working together • Nurturing opportunities for shared work					
24. Team Effort	• Creating group synergy in pursuing collective goals • Modeling team qualities like respect, helpfulness and cooperation • Building team identity, esprit de corps and commitment • Protecting the group and its reputation • Sharing credit • Putting team success above personal achievement					

Global Ethical Competence

How we see the Earth and all life on it as a web of delicate connections requiring stewardship for sustainability

Connections	How we act as part of a complex interconnected whole	Always in Place: 10-9 Usually in Place: 8-7 Sometimes in Place: 6-5 Rarely in Place: 4-3 Never in Place: 2-1				
Characteristic	**Explanation**	10 -9	8- 7	6- 5	4- 3	2- 1
25. Interdepend- ence	• Understanding our connections to each other and the Earth • Searching continuously for connections • Seeking always to see the big picture, taking the impact of your actions throughout the system into consideration • Seeking to practice systems thinking					
26. Stewardship	• Understanding our responsibility for future generations and acting with concern for their well-being • Acting with concern for sustainability • Seeking to understand natural ecosystems and nurture their well-being • Being fully mindful of our shared place in the natural world • Looking after your corner of the world, piece of land, business, etc.					
27. Global Citizenship	• Understanding our responsibility to act as citizens of the Earth • Acting locally but thinking globally • Being willing to sacrifice local short-term benefits for global long-term benefits • Being concerned about the well-being of all peoples in the Global System • Promoting fair trade practices globally • Being unwilling to participate in the exploitation of people from other places					

Global Ethical Competence Cont'd.

Future Orientation	How we act as responsible participants in creating a mutually beneficial future	Always in Place: 10-9 Usually in Place: 8-7 Sometimes in Place: 6-5 Rarely in Place: 4-3 Never in Place: 2-1				
Characteristic	**Explanation**	10-9	8-7	6-5	4-3	2-1
28. Future Orientation	• Seeing that actions today create the future tomorrow • Being guided by a vision of what is worth doing • Working with others to create a shared vision • Caring about the legacies you leave for future generations • Looking forward in a positive way to the future					
29. Visioning Strategically	• Scanning for strategy to achieve the result in the future that serves the greater good • Acting with deliberation to achieve the outcome that serves the common good					
30. Action Planning	• Connecting strategic vision to a plan of action • Laying out parallel and sequential action steps • Following through to achieve the worthwhile outcome • Being flexible to change the plan to fit new circumstances while maintaining commitment to the ethical vision.					

Total Score out of 300	
Divide by 3 to get the Ethical Quotient	
EthQ =	

Add the total value of your numbers from items 1-30

Divide this number by 3 to get the EthQ

Value _____ ÷ 3 = ——————→ EthQ = _____

Strengths and Areas for Development

From the above items, list the top three ethical competencies and the three areas most in need of development.

Strengths: #_____   #_____   #_____

Areas for Development: #_____   #_____   #_____

Personal Thoughts or Comments:

Personal Record Form
Ethical Competence Scale

Personal Ethical Competence

Foundational Characteristics   **Value Chosen**

1.   Trustworthiness   _____
2.   Conscientiousness   _____
3.   Consistency   _____
4.   Steadfastness   _____
5.   Integrity   _____
6.   Transparency   _____

Action Characteristics

7.   Learning Oriented   _____
8.   Courage   _____
9.   Determination   _____
10.   Optimism   _____
11.   Initiative   _____
12.   Thoroughness   _____

Social Ethical Competence

Empathy

13.   Understanding Others   _____
14.   Respecting Others   _____
15.   Caring About Others   _____
16.   Developing Others   _____
17.   Serving Others   _____

Social Skills

18.   Communication   _____
19.   Conflict Management   _____
20.   Inspiration   _____
21.   Building Bonds   _____
22.   Cooperation   _____
23.   Collaboration   _____
24.   Team Effort   _____

Global Ethical Competence

Connections

25.   Interdependence   _____
26.   Stewardship   _____
27.   Global Citizenship   _____

Future Orientation

28.   Future Orientation   _____
29.   Strategic Visioning   _____
30.   Action Planning   _____

                                TOTAL_____

Divide by 3 = EthQ   _____

Ethical Leadership Scale

Ethical Leadership Scale

Introduction

The Ethical Leadership Scale measures the qualities or characteristics of the ethical leader.

The ethical leader recognizes that the world as we know it is an outcome of human thought and action. It is far from perfect and therefore leaves room for continuous improvement. This gap between what is and what might be is what motivates the ethical leader to act. Anchoring effort in key principles of conduct and behavior, the ethical leader works with others to raise the quality of interactions among people and between humanity and the natural world. In doing this, the ethical leader displays qualities or characteristics in three sets of relationships:

1.   **Relationship to Self**: Personal qualities of the ethical leader

2.   **Relationship to Others**: Qualities that allow the ethical leader to connect with and empower others

3.   **Relationship to the Whole**: Qualities that reveal the ethical leader's sense of connection with the whole enterprise and with a grand design and high purpose.

Together the forty items on this Scale provide a thorough, representative description of an individual's mindstate (consciousness) and characteristic actions (behavior). It is a measure that reflects the current state of a person's competence as an ethical leader at the time the test is taken.

How to Use the Scale

To complete the Ethical Leadership Scale read the introduction and following comments carefully, so that you understand the purpose, assumptions and construction of the scale.

Consider each item and its explanations thoughtfully. Base your score value category selection on an honest perusal of your current thoughts and actions about yourself as a leader. Once you have selected a score value category, review the various ways in which this characteristic is described. If one of the aspects is weaker than the others, choose the lower of the two numbers in that score value category. If two items are weaker, choose the higher number in the score value category below. If more than two are weaker, choose the score value category below your first choice.

For example: 'Acts with integrity'. You have chosen *'usually in place' (8 or 7)*. However, you can think of instances where you have not maintained loyalty to those not present. You would then choose the lower number *(7)* for the value. As you consider further, you can remember several instances where you have not apologized sincerely. You would then go to the higher number of the score value category below, (*'sometimes in place'*). You would then have a value of *6*. If after further consideration you think that any other of the explanations are not usually the way you act or feel, you may want to reconsider the category you chose first and answer, *'sometimes in place' (6-5)*.

After you have considered each of the forty items separately and have recorded a value for each, add up your score out of 400 and divide by four to get the EthLQ. Record this number in the correct space. Then consider your personal strengths and areas for improvement and record them in the space provided. Finally, copy all of your scores onto the Personal Record Form for quick reference at a later time.

Remember, this Quotient is a reflection of your thinking to this time. It is not a fixed value. Doing this test should make you more aware of your characteristic mindstate and actions. This is the beginning of all change and growth. Or, you may be very satisfied with your current mindstate and doing this test will serve to affirm your thought and action.

Use the following Score Values to record the nature of your thinking and actions at this time.

This characteristic is:	
Always in place	10-9
Usually in place	8-7
Sometimes in place	6-5
Rarely in place	4-3
Never in place	2-1

Ethical Leadership Scale

Relationship to Self	Personal qualities of the ethical leader	Always in Place: 10-9 Usually in Place: 8-7 Sometimes in Place: 6-5 Rarely in Place: 4-3 Never in Place: 2-1				
Characteristic	Explanation	10 -9	8- 7	6- 5	4- 3	2- 1
1. Acts with Integrity	• Keeps promises and commitments and expects others to keep theirs • Maintains loyalty to those not present • Apologizes sincerely • Acts with honesty • Takes responsibility and cleans up after mistakes					
2. Trustworthy	• Can be thoroughly trusted • Is reliable and dependable • Is true to one's word • Is worthy of confidence					
3. Authentic	• Is consistently genuine in thought and action • Is honest and transparent • Recognizes that rules are important but not sufficient • Is real through and through					
4. Humble	• Is secure in the knowledge that one doesn't have all the answers • Is free from pretence or vanity • Keeps the ego in check • Is not boastful or aggressive about one's own qualities					
5. Intuitive	• Is willing to listen to the inner voice • Has a sense of the unknowable • Is guided by a faculty beyond reason • Acts on gut feeling of what is right to do					
6. Visionary	• Thinks big and new • Inspires a shared vision • Excites the collective imagination • Believes that dreams can become reality • Sees beyond the horizon • Acts as steward of the shared vision					

Relationship to Self Cont'd.	Personal qualities of the ethical leader	Always in Place: 10-9 Usually in Place: 8-7 Sometimes in Place: 6-5 Rarely in Place: 4-3 Never in Place: 2-1				
Characteristic	Explanation	10-9	8-7	6-5	4-3	2-1
7. Hopeful	• Maintains belief in positive outcome • Anchors optimism in considered action • Expects that right action will prevail • Does not despair in the face of adversity					
8. Creative	• Believes that life is a creative process • Opens the mind for creative insight • Believes that creativity gives meaning to life • Keeps the light of creative imagination burning • Is open to new and nontraditional ideas • Is entrepreneurial and energetic • Loves original and new ideas					
9. Patient	• Takes time to listen • Suspends judgment • Does not act impetuously • Waits for things to come together • Holds out for better outcome					
10. Confident	• Believes in one's ability to make a difference • Acts with assurance of purpose and intent • Has no doubt about securing good outcome • Believes in oneself and one's ability to succeed					
11. Clear Communicator	• Clarifies expectations • Seeks to understand others • Listens with empathy • Listens deeply and attentively • Does not deliver mixed messages					
12. Learning Oriented	• Is continuously learning • Keeps a teachable mind • Looks out for new learning opportunities and experiences • Searches for mentors • Is excited about and energized by learning					

Relationship to Self Cont'd.	Personal qualities of the ethical leader	Always in Place: 10-9 Usually in Place: 8-7 Sometimes in Place: 6-5 Rarely in Place: 4-3 Never in Place: 2-1				
Characteristic	Explanation	10-9	8-7	6-5	4-3	2-1
13. Open-Minded	• Keeps an open mind to all possibilities • Scans the horizon • Accepts new and conflicting information • Does not foreclose on options prematurely • Is willing to change one's mind when new information is presented					
14. Thinks Clearly	• Has a clear ability to conceptualize • Pays acute attention • Can clearly describe thoughts verbally • Is a good critical thinker • Sustains a wide span of awareness					
15. Knowledge-able	• Has a broad world view • Has a deep knowledge of one's specific field of expertise • Knows a lot about many things • Keeps up with developments					
16. Flexible	• Is not bound to fixed procedures • Is able to adapt quickly to new situations • Is willing to change one's mind based on information or opinion considered credible and worthy					
17. Attuned	• Very sensitive to others around them • Pays close attention to detail • Deeply empathetic					
18. Proactive	• Takes the initiative • Seeks to meet difficulties head on • Expects good outcome • Moves ahead without unnecessary delay					

Relationship to Self Cont'd.	Personal qualities of the ethical leader	Always in Place: 10-9 Usually in Place: 8-7 Sometimes in Place: 6-5 Rarely in Place: 4-3 Never in Place: 2-1				
Characteristic	Explanation	10 -9	8- 7	6- 5	4- 3	2- 1
19. Displays Positive Energy	• Is encouraging and positive towards others • Sees the good in each situation • Is a pleasure to be around • Is enthusiastic and optimistic					
20. Adventurous	• Sees life as a daring adventure • Looks forward to new experiences • Embraces change and innovation • Is willing to risk • Is enthusiastic about the new and the unknown					
21. Courageous	• Is brave and willing to act, even when afraid • Acts with sustained initiative • Is not dismayed by obstacles • Stands up to the bad stuff • Stands firm against the winds of resistance • Is willing to take the blame					
22. Has High Self-Esteem	• Knows that one has strong leadership qualities • Appreciates one's weaknesses and deficiencies • Is able to withstand personal attacks • Willingly accepts constructive criticism • Does not crack under destructive criticism or disapproval • Is confident and grounded about oneself and one's abilities • Believes in one's own competence					
23. Focused on Meaning	• Continuously seeks for meaning in life • Believes that meaningful thought and action are paramount • Abhors shallowness of intent • Acts with intention					

Relationship to Self Cont'd.	Personal qualities of the ethical leader	Always in Place: 10-9 Usually in Place: 8-7 Sometimes in Place: 6-5 Rarely in Place: 4-3 Never in Place: 2-1				
Characteristic	Explanation	10-9	8-7	6-5	4-3	2-1
24. Believes in Greatness	• Believes that greatness matters • Maintains a sustaining spirit • Has a sense of noble calling • Believes that life is meant to be heroic • Searches for higher ground • Has a sense of grace • Understands what is important					
25. Holds a Sense of Destiny	• Holds a sense of being called for higher purpose • Believes that leadership is a calling • Has a desire for legacy					

Relationship to Others	Qualities that allow the ethical leader to connect with and empower others	Always in Place: 10-9 Usually in Place: 8-7 Sometimes in Place: 6-5 Rarely in Place: 4-3 Never in Place: 2-1				
Characteristic	**Explanation**	10 -9	8- 7	6- 5	4- 3	2- 1
26. Compassion-ate	• Caring and empathetic • Is sympathetic to the needs of others • Does not turn away from helping others • Acts from a good heart as well as a firm resolve • Treats people with genuine affection					
27. Fair	• Treats others in an even-handed way • Does not court favorites • Tries to be reasonable • Considers issues on their merits • Is not prejudiced against race, gender, age, etc.					
28. Democratic	• Provides opportunities for free expression of opinion • Aims to provide equality of opportunity • Expects good ideas to emerge from all levels • Seeks widely for input on decisions					
29. Focused on Service	• Has a keen desire to serve others • Seeks to be helpful and charitable • Looks out for others • Treats others as one would wish to be treated by them • Understands that one is a servant first and leader second					
30. Focused on Relationships	• Is a good mentor or coach • Reaches out to others • Embraces systems of relationships • Sees the nurturing of relationships as an important part of embracing interdependence • Works continuously to sustain relationships while maintaining principles					

Relationship to Others	Qualities that allow the ethical leader to connect with and empower others	Always in Place: 10-9 Usually in Place: 8-7 Sometimes in Place: 6-5 Rarely in Place: 4-3 Never in Place: 2-1				
Characteristic	Explanation	10 -9	8- 7	6- 5	4- 3	2- 1
31. Believes in the Worth of Others	• Recognizes the rich resources in the minds and spirits of others • Believes in other people • Acts with regard for the other • Believes in mutuality and reciprocity					
32. Synergistic	• Thinks win-win • Holds an abundance mentality • Fosters creative cooperation • Enlists the compounding energy of full collaboration • Seeks to build an enthusiastic consensus • Looks for potential partners					
33. Encourages Teamwork	• Works to secure unity of thought, purpose and action • Participates actively at all levels • Inspires everyone to be on side and work together • Recognizes and applauds collective effort • Never fails to be a cheerleader of group effort • Is willing to both lead and follow					
34. Acts As a Model and Motivator of Others	• Models the way • Motivates others to want to struggle for shared aspirations • Takes people to places they have never been before • Is noted for clarity and persuasiveness of ideas • Says: "I'm going ... follow me." • Lifts people up to grow together					

Relationship to Others	Qualities that allow the ethical leader to connect with and empower others	Always in Place: 10-9 Usually in Place: 8-7 Sometimes in Place: 6-5 Rarely in Place: 4-3 Never in Place: 2-1				
Characteristic	**Explanation**	10-9	8-7	6-5	4-3	2-1
35. Nurtures Others	• Seeks to help others to make a meaningful contribution • Looks after others • Recognizes individual contributions • Celebrates the accomplishments of others • Consciously designs a learning process to enable others to develop					
36. Believes in Human Dignity	• Seeks always to uplift others • Disciplines without diminishing • Appreciates the importance of self-worth • Is always respectful of others					
37. Focused on Reality	• Keeps an eye on the details • Understands that competence is essential • Keeps an eye on the bottom line • Reminds others to stay focused on details as well as vision					

Relationship to the Whole	Qualities that reveal the ethical leader's sense of connection with a grand design and a higher purpose	Always in Place: 10-9 Usually in Place: 8-7 Sometimes in Place: 6-5 Rarely in Place: 4-3 Never in Place: 2-1				
Characteristic	**Explanation**	10 -9	8- 7	6- 5	4- 3	2- 1
38. Tolerates Contradiction and Anxiety	• Is able to live with contradiction • Is prepared to wait for closure • Is able to tolerate large amounts of anxiety • Understands that contradiction and anxiety can be the accompaniments of creative growth					
39. Systems Thinker	• Sees oneself and what one does as part of self-organizing systems • Sees life as an indivisible whole; one can't do right in one department while attempting to do wrong in another • Has a feel for underlying patterns • Understands that linear approaches to complex problems may not work • Sees the relationships between the parts and the whole					
40. Ecologically Conscious	• Sees humanity and all living things as part of an indivisible whole • Sees the ecosystems of the natural world as models for human designed systems • Understands the natural world as a model for cooperation and co-evolution • Understands how individual parts act together to make a whole environment • Is a champion and steward of the environment					

Total Score out of 400 [ ]

Divide by 4 to get the Ethical Leadership Quotient [ ]

EthLQ = [ ]

Add the total value of your numbers from items 1-40

Divide this number by 4 to get the EthLQ

Value _____ ÷ 4 = ———————▶ EthQ = _____

Strengths and Areas for Development

From the above items, list the top three ethical leadership competencies and the three areas most in need of development.

Strengths: #_____   #_____   #_____

Areas for Development: #_____   #_____   #_____

Personal Thoughts or Comments:

Personal Record Form
Ethical Leadership Scale

Relationship to Self	Value Chosen	Relationship to Others	Value Chosen
1. Acts with Integrity	_____	26. Compassionate	_____
2. Trustworthy	_____	27. Fair	_____
3. Authentic	_____	28. Democratic	_____
4. Humble	_____	29. Focused on Service	_____
5. Intuitive	_____	30. Focused on Relationships	_____
6. Visionary	_____	31. Believes in the Worth of Others	_____
7. Hopeful	_____	32. Synergistic	_____
8. Creative	_____	33. Encourages Teamwork	_____
9. Patient	_____	34. Acts As a Model and Motivator of Others	_____
10. Confident	_____	35. Nurtures Others	_____
11. Clear Communicator	_____	36. Believes in Human Dignity	_____
12. Learning Oriented	_____		
13. Open-Minded	_____	**Relationship to the Whole**	
14. Thinks Clearly	_____	37. Focused on Reality	_____
15. Knowledgeable	_____	38. Tolerates Contradiction and Anxiety	_____
16. Flexible	_____	39. Systems Thinker	_____
17. Attuned	_____	40. Ecologically Conscious	_____
18. Proactive	_____		
19. Displays Positive Energy	_____		
20. Adventurous	_____		
21. Courageous	_____		
22. Has high Self-Esteem	_____		
23. Focused on Meaning	_____		
24. Believes in Greatness	_____		
25. Holds a Sense of Destiny	_____		

TOTAL   _____

Divide by 4 = EthLQ   _____

Ethical Organization Scale

Ethical Organization Scale

Introduction

The hallmark of modern society is the way it is organized so that work gets done. By and large we live and work in social institutions, in organizations (private and public) and in communities (local, provincial, national and global). Each of these groupings has an effect on the people inside its boundaries, and the group's actions and behavior affect the larger community in which it is embedded. Together these social entities affect every aspect of our lives as well as the condition of the natural world on which we all depend. Moreover, each entity is connected in intricate ways to the web of the whole.

To the degree that the products, services and relationships that result from these groupings have a positive impact, our lives are improved and enhanced. If the impact is negative, our lives are diminished.

The purpose of the Ethical Organization Scale is to provide a measure of how, from an ethical perspective, the organizations in which we work affect the communities in which they operate. The measure is limited to an organization that you as the participant are familiar with. You are asked to choose an organization with which you are closely associated and where you have or would like to have a leadership role, now or in the past. The items in the scale are meant to describe a representative set of relationships in the larger picture. This will allow you to consider a particular organization as well as to gain an appreciation more generally for how organizations affect the communities in which they operate.

The ethical organization makes a positive contribution to its workforce, contractors, suppliers, customers (or clients), community, region, country and the planet. It is a community of people sharing and working together in an environment where they grow personally, feel fulfilled, contribute to a common good, and share in the personal, emotional and financial rewards of a job well done.

In order for you to provide a measure of how well the organization of your choice is doing from an ethical perspective, the Ethical Organization Scale is divided into the following sections:

1. Economic considerations: How it contributes economically

2. Relationships with the workforce: How relationships are handled within the organization

3. Relationships with contractors and suppliers: How it manages its relationships with external contractors and suppliers

4. Relationships with customers and clients: How it treats its customers or clients

5. Relationships with the community: How it behaves as a corporate citizen within the community

6. Relationships with the state/province, country and the world: How it acts in the provincial/state, national and global contexts

7. Ecological relationships: How it operates in relationship to the natural world

8. Cultural relationships: How it observes cultural norms

9. Social responsibility: How it manages its social responsibilities

10. Holistic perspective: How it takes a holistic perspective in relation to the greater good.

Together the ten items on this scale provide a representative description of how a particular organization operates from an ethical perspective, according to your assessment, at the time the instrument is used.

How to Use the Scale

To complete the Ethical Organization Scale read the introduction and following comments carefully, so that you understand the purpose, assumptions and construction of the scale.

Consider each item and its explanations thoughtfully. Base your score value category selection on an honest consideration of your experience with the organization.

Once you have selected a score value category, review the various ways in which the factor is described. If one of the aspects is weaker than the others, choose the lower of the two numbers in that score value category. If two items are weaker, choose the higher number in the score value category below. If more than two are weaker, choose the score value category below your first choice.

For example: 'Economic Considerations'. You have chosen *'usually'* (8 or 7). However, you can think of instances where the organization has not paid appropriate remuneration to its workforce. You would then choose the lower number *(7)* for the value. As you consider further, you can think of instances where the workforce has not benefited appropriately when the organization showed good profits. You would then go to the higher number of the score value category below, (*'sometimes'*). You would then have a value of 6. If after further consideration you think that any other of the explanations are not usually the way the organization acts, you may want to reconsider the category you chose first and answer, *'sometimes' (6-5).*

After you have considered each of the ten items separately and have recorded a value for each, add up your score out of 100 to get the EthOQ. Record this number in the correct space. Then consider the strengths of the organization and areas for improvement and record them in the space provided. Finally, copy all of your scores onto the Personal Record Form for quick reference at a later time.

Remember, this Quotient reflects your assessment of the organization's behavior at this time. It is not a fixed value. Doing this test should make you more aware of the organization's characteristic culture and actions. This is the beginning of all change and growth. Or, you may be very satisfied with the organization's current behavior and doing this test will serve to affirm it.

Use the following Score Values to record the nature of the organization's behavior at this time.

This characteristic is displayed:	
Always	10-9
Usually	8-7
Sometimes	6-5
Rarely	4-3
Never	2-1

Ethical Organization Scale

Relationships in an Ethical Organization	Qualities of an ethical organization	Always Displayed: 10-9 Usually Displayed: 8-7 Sometimes Displayed: 6-5 Rarely Displayed: 4-3 Never Displayed: 2-1				
Factor	**Explanation**	10-9	8-7	6-5	4-3	2-1
1. Economic Considerations	• Is financially successful • Its products and services make a positive contribution to the economy • Pays the appropriate taxes • Provides appropriate remuneration to members of its workforce • Allows its workforce to benefit from strong profits with shares, bonuses and/or salary adjustments • Provides products and / or services of value and of high quality					
2. Relationships with the Workforce	• Creates a safe, healthy, attractive work environment for its workforce • Treats members of the workforce with dignity and respect • Provides fair and equal opportunity for advancement without regard for ethnicity, gender, age or other distinctions • Provides physical and mental health support for members of the workforce • Provides meaningful work • Encourages self-development for members of its workforce					
3. Relationships with Contractors and Suppliers	• Pays contractors and suppliers fairly and on time • Provides a fair transparent bidding system for new contracts • Responds courteously and promptly to questions from contractors and suppliers • Provides all necessary information and feedback to contractors and suppliers					

Relationships in an Ethical Organization	Qualities of an ethical organization	Always Displayed: 10-9 Usually Displayed: 8-7 Sometimes Displayed: 6-5 Rarely Displayed: 4-3 Never Displayed: 2-1				
Factor	Explanation	10-9	8-7	6-5	4-3	2-1
4. Relationships with Customers or Clients	• Describes products and services fairly and truthfully • Provides high quality and high value goods and services • Provides what it says it will provide • Responds quickly and appropriately to complaints or problems • Treats customers or clients with dignity and respect • Is accurate and truthful in all communications and advertising					
5. Relationships with the Community	• Acts responsibly to do no harm in the community • Abides honestly and without subterfuge or intimidation to local rules and regulations • Considers the community in providing employment, i.e. seeks to provide good jobs to members of the community and acts responsibly towards the community if it needs to move jobs or business elsewhere					
6. Relationships with the State/ Province, Country and the World	• Works responsibly within regulatory frameworks • Is socially responsible to workers in other nations • If manufacturing abroad, does not participate in exploitation of extra national workers by paying low wages or by employment of children or by operating with unhealthy or unsafe working conditions • Does not export a product or service that could harm people or the environment in other countries • Does not produce a product or service that could harm the health or well-being of people locally or abroad					

Relationships in an Ethical Organization	Qualities of an ethical organization	Always Displayed: 10-9 Usually Displayed: 8-7 Sometimes Displayed: 6-5 Rarely Displayed: 4-3 Never Displayed: 2-1				
Factor	Explanation	10-9	8-7	6-5	4-3	2-1
7. Ecological Relationships	• Does no harm to the local environment • Works to support sustainability as it does its business • Takes time and makes the necessary effort to understand delicate ecological relationships to ensure that it does not harm them					
8. Cultural Relationships	• Respects the culture and traditions of the communities where it operates as long as they are consistent with universally recognized standards • Provides support to cultural activities where this is appropriate • Seeks opportunities to enhance cultural development					
9. Social Responsibility	• Recognizes that it has a social responsibility to be a good corporate citizen wherever it operates • Seeks opportunities to contribute to good causes and charitable initiatives • Seeks to improve conditions in society where it can					
10. Holistic Perspective	• Sees itself as part of a seamless web of relationships • Understands the interconnectedness of what it does with other parts of the social/cultural/ecological environment and seeks to maintain positive and supportive relationships for mutual benefit					

Total Score out of 100 [   ]

EthOQ = [   ]

Add the total value of your numbers from items 1-10

EthOQ = _____

Strengths and Areas for Development

From the above items, list the top three factors and the three factors most in need of development.

Strengths:　　　　　　　　　#_____　　#_____　　#_____

Areas for Development:　　#_____　　#_____　　#_____

Personal Thoughts or Comments:

Personal Record Form
Ethical Organization Scale

Factor		Value Chosen
1.	Economic Considerations	_____
2.	Relationship with the workforce	_____
3.	Relationships with contractors and suppliers	_____
4.	Relationships with customers or clients	_____
5.	Relationships with the community	_____
6.	Relationships with the State/Province, Country and the World	_____
7.	Ecological relationships	_____
8.	Cultural relationships	_____
9.	Social responsibility	_____
10.	Holistic perspective	_____

TOTAL _____

EthOQ _____

PART 2

Perspectives on Ethical Leadership

Ethical Leadership

The leader has always been an essential part of any human community. Fortunes, customs, laws, governance, religion all derive from dominant leadership. Some leadership comes from the sword. All leadership is of the word. Many leaders stand on pinnacles of power. Others work from less lofty platforms. Leadership spans all ages, from children in school to elders at the council table. No gathering is too small or too large to call for leadership. No agenda too onerous or too simple. Wherever people are, there we will find the leaders. Some derive their leadership from office, others from their person, most from their expertise. For leaders must stand apart, at least for a time, and thereby declare they are in charge.

The strength and quality of a society derives from its leadership. The most successful do not require their leaders to be a burning ray or to light innumerable fires of achievement. Such societies may flourish for a while, but like the fires will quickly burn out. When leadership is dispersed in the minds of all the people, then bands of steel are forged; for strong leadership is a quality of the whole, commingling in ever changing patterns, and deriving its essential greatness from principles shared at the core.

History grand and modest has seen it all: communities, groups and nations who have thrown in their lots with a dominant leadership and reaped the harvest or the whirlwind for their choice; vision and foresight energized around a noble ideal or wasted on ill-fated ambition. For human character is a flux of contradictions. It can falter as often as it triumphs. The true spark of enlightened leadership is seen when it ignites our noblest passion and lights the pathway of the quest for higher purpose.

Such then is what we call ethical leadership. It takes the other shining qualities of vision, courage, expertise and determination and gives them the rock solid platform on which to stand. It is leadership that goes beyond the rationality of mind and the warmth of heart to the integrity of soul. It is leadership distilled from the highest moral precepts of the world's great traditions of wisdom and spirituality. At its heart is trust. Its mantle is honesty. Steadfast reliability is its face.

Such leadership commands respect, not just for the content of its policy, but also for the trustworthiness of its action. Ethical leadership always takes the path to justice. It seeks not to distribute favors to a few, but benefits to many, justly earned by the quality of their effort. It keeps commitments and it honors loyalty, when in its judgment effort is in the direction of right action.

Ethical leaders are strong, generous, full-hearted, trustworthy, resolute and utterly reliable. They will not be without error or fault, but they will be honest in the admission of their fault when they have searched in their soul and seen it. They will not seek to dominate, except when they see the core principles of right action are in danger. They will encourage others to come forward when it is their turn to lead. They will seek to guide rather than to direct. Their greatest achievements are made when the people move forward on their own.

Human heritage has bequeathed to citizens of the third millennium many leadership qualities. Of these, four stand out: vision, courage, expertise and ethics. All four are important. But only one is essential. Ethical leadership anchors all the rest.

Leadership in the First Decade of the Millennium

We are truly living in an unprecedented time, an age in which an evolved human consciousness is in the process of changing the world. Co-existing as one part of a whole spectrum of human consciousness, from the most primitive to the most advanced, this surge of new thinking raises compelling questions about the kind of leadership the world needs as the third millennium begins. In essence, the challenge is to link together the growing cohort of thinkers whose wise stewardship can lead this planet to a place where an evolved species of *Homo sapiens sapiens* can flourish in an historic safe harbor.

To join this cohort requires credentials of a different kind from those that appear on walls as diplomas granted by institutions of higher learning. The credentials of the new leaders will be evident through acts of courage, through modeling right action even in the face of risk, through dedicated loyalty, integrity and great enthusiasm for the group's raison d'être.

To become such a leader, one needs to focus on the journey itself, how the game of life and work is played, and not only on the destination or the bottom line. At the same time, such a leader keeps the end in mind, expects an outstanding outcome, uses rigorous rational thinking, and especially focuses on the big picture, even while mired in the daily blur of detail.

To be such a leader one needs to understand how to generate, nurture and sustain outstanding performance in oneself and others. The emphasis must be on the prime skill of achieving difficult goals. Such leaders need to know what strategies and safeguards are required to produce outstanding results with ordinary people.

> *Which leads us to investigate the power of relationships to*
> *create within individuals the ability to perform at such high*
> *levels, and within teams, to achieve seemingly impossible goals.*

The Power of Relationships

To understand the power of relationships, we need to consider what our current scientific knowledge of the nature of consciousness says about the very fabric of our humanity.

We are beginning to revise our understanding of who we are as human beings and what we are made of. We know now that we are not material entities with fixed physical limits like machines, but rather we are energy systems undergoing dynamic, continuous renewal. We are not a body, a mind and a spirit, but a whole living being in which all systems are interconnected and entirely governed by mind. Significantly, that mind is not only in the head, but in every cell of the body, so integrated and exquisitely tuned that a single thought produces a flood of neurochemical action that either engages or depresses action instantly. Even questions of health, and indeed life and death, can now be answered by our understanding of how the mind affects the immune system's response to its challenges.

Cloaked with this exquisite human organism, we are also attuned to each other, such that the whole of us responds with extraordinary sensitivity to each other, in both physical and mental ways, whether we intend this to happen or not.

Thus, it is in the relationships between us that the power of outstanding performance lies. The championship team, the outstanding business success, events of personal, national and international heroism or greatness—all are fully dependent on the elusive spirit of relationships within the team. The reason for this lies in the nature of who we are and what we need in order to function effectively.

Safe Harbor and Clarity of Purpose

All human beings need safe harbor to do their best work. To have this they must be able to trust the people close to them. Along with trust comes a sense of dignity, respect and encouragement, supported by a conviction that honesty, justice, fairness and integrity govern the actions of the group. Without this people enter the forum of daily activity with the need to protect themselves, to look after their own case, which detracts from whatever focus they need to do their work.

Once safe harbor is achieved, people need to be energized by clarity of purpose, a feeling that the job they are doing is important and that it is right that they do it. Indeed, they must be so convinced of its importance and rightness that they will risk courageously to achieve it. They must personally be part of the action. They need to have a role to play, to be counted on for their individual competent contribution. They need to know that the team is counting on them and expects them to do their best.

Related to this is the power of creativity. The creative impulse to invent new responses when old solutions are not producing the best result must be enthusiastically supported even in the face of potential temporary failure.

> *Which leads us then to ask how all this is related to leadership.*
> *How can a leader generate such spirit in others, and nurture and*
> *sustain it to respond effectively to the challenges of the new times?*

Begin with Oneself

The answer emerges with starling simplicity—begin with oneself. To engender trust a leader must be trustworthy. To promote justice, one must be just; to engage enthusiasm, be enthusiastic. In other words, a leader must model all the qualities and characteristics he or she expects of others. To coach, one must know how to play the game oneself. Indeed, such leadership demands that we never ask others to do something we are unwilling to do ourselves.

Those who would develop leaders for a new time must be ready to walk their talk, to go first into risk, while at the same time being ready to double back and bring up the rear, if that is where the greater danger lies. Through all this action, the leader will pay constant attention to the relationships with each member of the team, providing new access when necessary, always ensuring that the relationships among the team members model the leader's relationships with them. This includes healthy competitiveness for place and promotion, so long as the overall safety of the unit is preserved by everyone accepting that responsibility.

Which leads us to rethink what we mean by a hero.

The New Hero

From antiquity and through history, the title and respect of hero has gone to the conqueror—to Alexander, to Caesar, to Napoleon, to Peter the Great. Mesmerized by their achievements, the world has thought less about the land they desecrated and the people they subjugated. Even in modern times wealth and power continue to be regarded as the criteria of greatness, regardless of the harm done to others in the pursuit of those ends.

However, as we move into the post-modern era, a new spirit is abroad that denies the acceptability of achieving greatness through doing harm to others. On the world stage in recent times, from the brutal leadership of the Serbs and Bosnians with their policies of ethnic cleansing, and the monstrous behavior of Saddam Hussein in the Middle East and the butchers in Rwanda, to the silent willingness of Swiss banks to profit from Nazi atrocities— all this is being exposed, challenged and denounced by the free world and its media. Closer to home in our own country, acting without integrity, or lying and cheating to win either in politics or sport is being challenged on every front. Within the largest or smallest enterprise, from the Department of Defense and monolithic power utilities to the local corner store or small business contractor, trustworthiness and integrity are demanded by the client or consumer of goods and services.

So we live now in a world of transition and the resulting confusion. We are reluctant to give up the tarnished heroes of the past, while we expect something different from the heroes of the present, but still remain fascinated by the scoundrels who masquerade as leaders in real life and who leap out at us daily from the disturbed imaginations of those who craft the mainstream stories of television and film.

Which brings us to the question: How then shall we live?

Choosing the Way

The person who chooses to live with emotional health in such a world as described above will find the way by joining the cohort of new leaders and new heroes who champion the cause of "right action" beginning with themselves. The reward for such leadership goes well beyond wealth, power or position. It comes from the opportunity to live a life of meaning, to make a difference, to leave the world better for the life you lived, to provide a better place for those who follow you.

Pushing your own potential to its limit allows you to transcend yourself as the energy system you know you surely are. If this is done in the direction of right action, you will live a healthy quality life. The relationships you model for others return to you to empower you in body-mind-spirit to produce the best of who you are.

Such rewards are priceless. Being on a life path that allows such traveling is the ultimate and most sacred human journey.

The Ethical Competence Framework

The requirements for success are changing. Individuals and organizations are being judged by measures at once as old as civil society but at the same time as new as the 21st century. No longer is it sufficient merely to generate a healthy financial bottom line, but increasingly we are being challenged to justify our success in terms of how well we support one another and how we care for the natural world on which all life depends.

The new measures are grounded in the age-old concept of ethics—the study of human conduct with emphasis on the determination of right and wrong. These principles lie at the core of all major spiritual traditions. They have been the gold standard for human behavior for millennia. But their application in modern economic industrialized society has been twisted and tangled in pursuit of another less noble principle—expediency: grasping for advantage rather than for what is right.

However, the 21st century is governed by a new watchword: interdependence. Economies and cultures are now so intertwined that the pursuit of advantage in one quarter based on self interest without due regard to its impact on others can set off a chain reaction that ultimately bedevils everyone. In this environment the old has become new again. The ethical rules of the past acquire a new and urgent prominence in the present. We are challenged as individuals, organizations and society to become ethically competent.

To be competent means having ability in sufficient measure that one can perform at an acceptable standard. These are all subjective terms. What is sufficient? How much is acceptable? What is the standard? The answers come slowly and tortuously out of conflict and consequences. The process is hard learning, and the question is always whether we will collectively learn fast enough and well enough to avoid the worst of the consequences.

We are therefore in the process of defining what it means to be ethically competent in an interdependent world. A further challenge is speed. In large measure local and global interdependence are driven by the speed of communications and the rapidity with which new knowledge replaces old. Under such conditions foundational beliefs of what is right or wrong become both urgent and important to avoid a precipitous slide into chaos.

Relationship to Emotional Competence

Ethical competence is closely associated with the concept of emotional competence, which determines how well we handle ourselves and each other. Groundbreaking work was done in the 1990s by Daniel Goleman on promoting emotional intelligence as the new yardstick for measuring success at work. Though Goleman did not forge the link between ethics and emotions very forcefully, it is clear that a case can be made for a concept of ethical intelligence giving rise to ethical competence as a step beyond showing how emotional intelligence determines success in the workplace and in society.

Goleman defined emotional competence as "a learned capability based on emotional intelligence that results in outstanding performance at work." Though difficult to measure, emotional intelligence is observable as the quality that distinguishes successful performance beyond training and expertise and high cognitive intelligence as measured by IQ tests.

Similarly, it can be argued that ethical competence is a learned capability based on ethical intelligence that results in smooth harmonious and peaceful relationships at every level in society. Like emotional competence it is difficult to measure, but its presence or absence in an individual, organization or society is readily observable. As we have witnessed in recent years high profile examples of ethical incompetence—from the Enron debacle in business to the tainted blood scandal in public health—we begin to wonder whether there is not some way that we can set a standard of ethical competence that leads to practices that are teachable and able to be learned and that would raise the level of ethical behavior at every level.

The Ethical Competence Framework

The Ethical Competence Framework provides a way to do this. It builds on the concept of the Emotional Competence Framework presented by Goleman in *Working with Emotional Intelligence* (New York: Bantam Books, 1998). The Ethical Competence Framework incorporates three dimensions of competence, beginning with the personal and moving through social competence to global competence. By including the last dimension recognition is given to the new imperative of life in the 21st century, namely, that the ultimate determinant of success for humanity is our ability to create a harmonious sustainable global civilization on a finite planet.

Each dimension of the Ethical Competence Framework is further divided into descriptive components that generate in total 30 items that are grouped into the Ethical Competence Scale. By assigning values from 1 to 10 for each of the 30 items a score can be obtained, which expressed as a percentage, becomes the Ethical Quotient (EthQ), following the tradition of expressing cognitive intelligence as the Intelligence Quotient or IQ.

No claim is made that the Ethical Quotient is an accurate or distinguishing measure between individuals or organizations on their level of ethical competence. However, the process of using the scale in combination with the Ethical Competence Framework provides a rigorous and effective teaching and learning tool that can move people singly and collectively towards understanding what is required for ethical competence.

High Stakes

More significant than the actual EthQ score is the information and reflection provided to those who use the Scale of their relative strengths in ethical competence and the areas where improvement is warranted. To the extent that all of us individually and collectively work to improve perceived ethical deficiencies in our behavior, so goes the future of the world. Most important of all is the need to incorporate strong ethical competence in powerful business, industrial and government organizations; otherwise we can face a horrendous future governed by fear and abuse of devastating power.

The stakes are high for humanity and all life on Earth. The ethical challenge has never been greater. The call is for ethical leadership to incorporate strong teaching on ethical competence at all levels in society and across the interdependent world.

Doing the Right Thing

It is a well known dictum in the executive world that leaders are the people who do the right thing and managers are the ones who do things right. The expression gets its power from the shades of meaning the word "right" has in the English language. To do "the right thing" means to make a choice among possibilities in favor of something the collective wisdom of humanity knows to be the way to act. To "do things right" carries the meaning of efficiency, effectiveness, expertise and the like. This does not mean leaders are inefficient or lack expertise, nor that managers know nothing about the big picture. It is simply a way of highlighting that a leader must call upon a broad band of intuitive knowledge and use it to give guidance and direction.

Two things are critical here. The first is we believe that somehow out of all the myriad of possibilities in a complex world there is something we can call "right action" in a given situation. The second is we believe someone, namely, the leader, will be able to find "the right thing" and choose to do it, no matter what. Both of these beliefs say much about why human affairs sometimes go so well, and why at other times they go very badly. If a person comes to a position of power as a leader in an organization or in society without knowing how to do the right thing, then the people under his or her influence are in for a bad time. At worst they will find themselves plunged into brutal conflict with outside forces, or at best they will spend a lot of time and energy struggling with internal disharmony and damage control.

That these kinds of mismatches and consequences occur all too frequently in human affairs should suggest to us we are doing something wrong. The simplistic answer is that we should select, appoint or elect better leaders. True, but the problem is we don't know how to do that, and, moreover, we tend to inherit many of our leaders through rights of birth, ownership, seniority, prestige, wealth, etc.

The more thoughtful approach to helping with our problem of ineffective leadership is to look to the basic assumption from which the problem comes. It is the first of the two beliefs mentioned above: that "right action" in a given situation is knowable. If we believe that, then we should examine the issue of how right action is knowable, rather than jump quickly to the second belief that there is a leader somewhere out there who will know what the right action is and do it for us. It is in handing off the responsibility for "doing the right thing" from ourselves to someone else that we get into trouble.

The reason we believe right action is knowable is that our human traditions are full of stories which tell us this is so. From the Judeo-Christian pronouncements of the Ten Commandments and their equivalent in other spiritual traditions, to the simple stories telling of good deeds, brave sacrifice, honest dealing, of our children's literature, we are brought up "knowing" there are right ways and wrong ways to act. If we widen the net to include stories from the political, military and business arenas, then we also know about how particular moves were made down through history that resulted in some notable achievement. Sometimes luck was involved, but always somewhere in the story a prepared mind knew how to "do the right thing."

And therein lies the clue to what is missing from our current efforts to promote right action in our society. We are not doing sufficient to prepare enough minds to know what right action is. A leader is not able to lead effectively if the people he or she is leading have not themselves learnt the lessons of right action. True, part of the role of the leader is to be a teacher and model of right action, but if the minds of the people are clouded by preoccupation with self-interest, the leader is more likely to be sacrificed than respected and followed.

What this brings us back to is the understanding that the quality and act of leadership must be distributed throughout society. We are each of us leaders in our own spheres of influence. What kind of leader we will be is determined by the quality of our leadership mind. Foremost among the attributes of that mind is the ability to know what is the "right thing" to do. If enough of us know that and practice it under the mentorship and guidance of those who choose to come forward into larger offices of leadership, then it is likely we will have a successful and just and decent society. If not, then we don't have much to look forward to.

All of this reinforces the point that ethics lie at the core of a successful society or organization, and that ethical leadership is one of our greatest continuing needs. It is no coincidence we say a leader is one who does "the right thing." We have seen all too frequently this century the misery and carnage which flow in the wake of unethical leadership. We are seeing today the moral fiber in our own peace-loving society warped and weakened by leaders in high places who do not do the right thing. But sadly they are to large degree poor products of our own inadequate efforts to place ethical teaching at the center point of who we are and what we stand for. Self-serving materialism has led us to treat each other and our beautiful planet and its wondrous life forms as objects to be exploited rather than as the living tissue of our own being. In our impassioned pursuit of technology and technique we have forgotten that life comes first.

So there is much to do to reshape the way we live together with right action at the core. We must find new ways of retelling the old stories of decency, love, cooperation and support. New heroes who create new myths of stewardship and service must displace the old warrior image and the screen idols who indulge their lives of violence and conquest in adventures on the dark side of humanity. We must let in the light in a hundred thousand ways to show how we can walk together into the future and know at every step we are trying hard to do the right thing.

Ethical Leadership:
The Applied Wisdom of the Feminine Perspective

Something happens inside a woman's consciousness when she gives birth to a child that forever changes the adolescent in her. She becomes the practical nurturer with every cell of her being. Talking about doing the right thing by the child is not enough. "Right action" must take place in response to an urgent agenda that is not her own. The baby must be fed, changed, comforted, and the nest made conducive to safety and growth twenty-four hours a day. She becomes an adult whose goodness is directed to ensuring the next generation prospers.

As the child grows, the mother becomes by necessity educator and mentor. Through the quality of her nurturing the next generation flourishes or fades, blooms or wanes. (I have left the father's role out of the discussion for the moment and will come back to it.) No one has called this activity leadership. Indeed it is this very preoccupation with children's early nurturing that has forced women into second class citizenship as leaders and champions. Yet every known tradition values this "right action" at the heart of its moral code, and finds some way to protect this process as the price of the tribe's or society's survival.

Looking across to the natural world, the same phenomenon of the female as nurturer is central to most species' survival. With our species it is more pronounced, because the human child is born helpless and requires several years of careful nurturing for its powerful brain to develop to full potential.

Lessons for Leadership

The nurturing phenomenon, whether personally experienced or culturally generated, makes women think differently from men about life and its meaning. As women increasingly sit in board rooms of corporations or government, as they experience high office and take charge of business, they bring this underlying perspective to the table, whether they recognize it or not. Schooled in the very essence of life's meaning, they bring a different perspective to decision making, which provides important lessons to those interested in ethical leadership.

The first lesson is that the process of life is essentially democratic. All mothers do this nurturing. The act transcends every barrier of language, race and class. It is the great equalizer. Thus women in general are readier to ascribe skill across the strata of the community, and do not assume that competence is dependent on rank or birth.

Secondly, women understand that survival is dependent on urgent action on a daily basis in tiny steps. They know that health is best managed by prevention--like proper food, sleep and nutrition--and they continually work from crisis to crisis as the vagaries of infection, injury and life's fortunes impact their family. From this they learn to get to the heart of it, to create a day from rising to sleeping that has some good in it. They do not delay or hold back the needed comfort.

The third lesson we can learn from the mother's perspective is to be continuously amazed and astounded by the child's intelligence and good sense that engenders both awe and respect for human life. This is translated by mothers into what they understand to be love and loving acts. It is this phenomenon which brings us to the very heart of the lessons to be learned from the female perspective on life.

We have been enjoined by the creators of our traditions, mostly masculine, to "love one another" without truly understanding what the word "love" means. The word has been robbed of any specific meaning by its widespread application to all kinds of feelings. Spiritual traditions use it. New Age thinking is awash in its use. Our culture uses it to sell every aspect of material life by promising it as reward for buying every product our imagination can conjure up. By such widespread use, no one dares speak against it, but few really know what it means to them.

However, mothers, whether they can give language to it or not, truly know that at the very basis of its meaning, love is the feeling of awe and respect for the loved one and indeed for all human life. That feeling is also directed at their mothers and sisters and themselves for having produced it. Somehow, because our society has devalued this phenomenon, the self esteem and respect and awe that is at the very source of life's survival has been distorted. Even so, women still bring this value to the table, often in spite of themselves.

What Does This Mean for Ethical Leadership?

When one strips away all the words, all the cultural overtrappings of every society, the value of awe and respect for life is at the very source of every positive emotion. Doing no harm to life, and nurturing it to the next seven generations has created the fundamental creed in every tradition. Wherever these values are distorted by the culture, humanity suffers. Fundamental to all this is the question that goes back one step further to the origin of everything: *How did all this incredible life and the planet needed for its sustenance come to be?*

The mystery generated by this wondering, despite current scientific explanations, goes to the core of our spirituality and begs the greater question: *Do we have the right to destroy what has been so divinely created?*

Thus, it is the respect and awe for life which is the basis of feminine consciousness, and life's task for the vast majority of us, is to empower the growth of that life to independent adulthood. What if we were to bring these feelings out into the open? What if we included them in the bottom line? What if we truly made them part of our decisions?

How then could we wage war, harm one another in business, and destroy the air, water and land along with the flora and fauna that sustain us?

These are not unworldly or idealistic questions. They are the most practical issues at the very base of reality. Of course a perfect response is not always possible, just as a child's need cannot always be fully met. We do the best we can, but we never knowingly go against the basic code, and we always keep the child's well-being in continuous consideration.

Now what about men? How do they figure in this equation? In this case people of my generation have something to learn from the young generation of men now becoming fathers. I observe my son and sons-in-law and those of my friends participating in active and important ways in every aspect of parenting, from the birth itself to the care and nurturing of the children. This is not about a new cultural phenomenon, but rather about masculine strength, which expresses the best of itself in its most noble form when it acts with gentleness in caring for and providing safe harbor to mother and child.

The ingredients that comprise this great soup of nurturing contain all the positive human values. Here we find the source of self-worth, of trust and trustworthiness, of integrity and authenticity. We need look no deeper than this common foundation of the world's cultures for an ethical transformation of an emerging global community. As we look at the essence of all communities, we shall find that their survival over time was dependent on the respect and awe for life of their members. Now, as global citizens of a global community, we must do no less on this broadest of all possible fronts.

This is the foundation on which we can build our new codes of life and law and business. On this life-giving principle we should build every new treaty. Considering this should be the basis of every new project. Indeed, if we finally did this, we could at last be proud of how we are handling the great heritage of life entrusted to us, and with equal pride hand it over to the generations that follow.

PART 3

Global Ethical Perspectives

Creating a Knowledge Society: The Building Blocks of a New Transcendent Humanity

This essay was prepared originally by Desmond Berghofer as a presentation for a Symposium on "Building Bridges: Towards a Sustainable Future for All" hosted by the Canadian Commission for UNESCO in Halifax, Canada on May 7, 2004

INTRODUCTION

The story of knowledge is the story of humanity. From ancient times to the postmodern age, across cultural borders and ethnic traditions, between traditional and technologically developed societies, the common currency is knowledge. To investigate, create, modify and change is endemic to human nature. Knowledge of all kinds floods into every crevice of our planet where *Homo sapiens*, the wise ones, have established a presence. The question for us today is not so much how to build a knowledge society, but how to combine the systems of knowledge we now have into a recipe that can intellectually nourish the human family towards a sustainable future.

The major challenge facing us is to create a global knowledge society that can sustain, in a reasonable quality of life, a world population estimated to reach nine billion people by 2050. The prospects that we will be able to achieve this goal do not look good. Already we are unable to sustain a global population of six and a half billion people so that most enjoy a decent standard of living, and, moreover, we are running into natural limits for what we are doing and for the way we are doing it.

The main reason for concern has much less to do with the creation of knowledge—humanity is very good at that—but rather with our unwillingness and seeming inability to take responsibility for how we apply knowledge.

The Human Dilemma

Our human dilemma has been described in some detail by Vaclav Havel, former President of the Czech Republic, who has emerged over the past decade as a respected, thoughtful and articulate commentator on the human condition. Speaking in 1997 at Forum 2000 to thirteen scholars from various disciplines, he said he hoped their deliberations would shed some light on what he finds to be a very troubling reality, namely, that humankind shows little determination to avert the threats about which it knows so much. By threats, he was referring to a litany that most of us know well: how to feed a world population with a still soaring growth rate; the difficulty of various nationalities and cultures to coexist crowded so dramatically together; the contribution of human activities to global warming, to the destruction of the environment and to disturbing the balance of ecosystems; the ongoing presence of nuclear weapons; the current and expected future rise of social problems, crime, drug abuse, terrorism and other forms of human alienation and frustration.

Vaclav Havel went on to comment that we do not seem to be perturbed by the evidence that the resources of this planet are limited and that demand is beginning to exhaust supply. On the contrary, rising production, and therefore also consumption, is sensed as the main sign of success by both poor and wealthy states, thereby "cutting the branch on which they are sitting by their ideology of stupidly indefinite and senseless growth."

That we have come to this place as we build the knowledge society ought to give us pause to wonder if perhaps we are doing something wrong.

Mr. Havel expressed his deep conviction that the only option for controlling what he called our "perpetual motion towards disaster" is for something to change in "the sphere of the spirit, in the sphere of human conscience, in the actual attitude of man towards the world and his understanding of himself and his place in the overall order of existence;" in other words, "to understand differently and more perfectly the true purpose of our existence."(1)

Conflict between the Knowledge Society and Sustainability

Clearly, the knowledge society we have built into the first decade of the 21st century is in conflict with sustainability. Therefore, if we are going to hold the two ideas, "knowledge society" and "sustainability" together in our minds we must begin to think about a very different kind of knowledge society than the one we have invented. We are not concerned here with a tinkering at the edges; we are faced with a profound rethinking of a dominant paradigm. We must replace a paradigm of growth and consumption with one that truly acknowledges our intimate connection to the natural world and our absolute interdependence across all boundaries of nationality and ethnicity as stewards of the Earth and custodians of the future.

Why is it so difficult for us to do this? The answer lies, at least in part, in the cultural myth that underlies the knowledge society. This creates the assumptions and flawed policies that push us into continuous crisis.

FLAWS OF THE KNOWLEDGE SOCIETY

Every new generation is born into a system of beliefs and knowledge on which it continues to build. Over time this coalesces into substantial change and current generations tend to look back dismissively to the knowledge systems of previous ages, not realizing the extent to which their own knowledge base is built at best on tenuous assumptions and at worst on flawed beliefs and outmoded cultural myths. The techno-industrial knowledge society of the 21st century suffers from many such flaws.

The Myth of Sustainability through Growth

Possibly the most serious illusion of our age is that we can achieve sustainability through growth. A forceful critic of this modern myth is William Rees, Professor of Community and Regional Planning at the University of British Columbia. "For the first time", he says, "the world seems to be converging on a common developmental ideology, one that promises ever-increasing wealth for everyone, everywhere."(2) This is the global vision that everyone can prosper through unlimited economic expansion fuelled by open markets and more liberalized trade. A key assumption is that continuously improving technology will be able to compensate for the depletion of any important natural resources. However, evidence of every kind is now showing that as national economies expand, the ecosphere degrades. Regrettably, overall human welfare does not seem to improve either, for the benefits of economic growth accrue mainly to the already wealthy. Moreover, it is the world's poor who suffer the most when ecosystems are degraded, while, ironically, the world's rich don't enjoy much measurable improvement from income growth, for "beyond a certain income level there is little indication of improvement in subjective assessments of well-being."(3)

Thus, we have a built-in economic imperative in our knowledge society to consume more and more of the Earth's resources for no great advantage. The only way that the world's wealthiest nations can live the way they do is by drawing on the ecological surpluses of other nations. As resources become scarcer, the process becomes geopolitically destabilizing. Mixed with ethnic, racial and religious tensions, and faced with the continuing reality of growth in world population, particularly in the poorer countries, it should be obvious that we are heading towards a future none of us would willingly choose to live in.

Higher Education is Part of the Problem

Regrettably, the flaws of the knowledge society described above are embedded in our systems of higher education. William Rees describes the situation succinctly: "Universities and colleges have been swept along all too passively by the winds of corporate globalization. The knowledge society is no longer a public good."(4) In Science and Engineering faculties, students learn that the world is a mechanistic place. Business and Commerce teach to maximize shareholder value. "The bulk of research goes to disciplines that create marketable intellectual property of every kind." The Humanities wither by comparison, and students are traumatized by the material culture in which they are embedded. "No one should be surprised that the result is the widespread erosion of community, the moral corruption of commerce, and the wholesale degradation of ecosystems, now on a global scale."(5)

A strong indictment indeed! Yet, a different kind of knowledge society can be created, which we shall come to shortly, but first we must understand some other problems and challenges.

Dancing with Systems

The mindset of our techno-industrial age is that somehow we can predict and control the natural world. An impassioned and eloquent voice expressing a contrarian view came from Donella Meadows, until her life was tragically cut short by illness a few years ago. Meadows was a college professor and systems analyst, and at the time of her death, was working on a book called Thinking in Systems. The book is to be published posthumously by the Sustainability Institute. Excerpts were published in the March/April 2004 issue of *Timeline* by The Foundation for Global Community.

Meadows warns us that "self-organizing non-linear feedback systems are inherently unpredictable. They are not controllable."(6) This speaks to another serious flaw in the knowledge society—a belief that we can approach the natural world, not as a participant, but as an omniscient conqueror. Obsessed with numbers, we feel that we can somehow manage the future. We focus on measuring and manipulating parts of the system, forgetting that the parts cannot survive without a healthy whole.

This belief has led us into the reductionist, discipline-centered knowledge system that is now getting us into so much trouble. Meadows reminds us that the mental models we carry around in our heads are just that—models of reality, which we must be prepared to challenge continuously. Her advice is that we must dance with the systems we find in the world, follow them across traditional disciplinary lines, and expand the horizons of what we care about, recognizing that "no part of the human race is separate, either from other human beings or from the global ecosystem."(7)

But how did we get into the trap of reductionist thinking in the first place? To understand this we must turn to the history of science.

The Science Story

The ground rules for science were set in the 17th century by René Descartes, who distinguished between two orders of reality. On the one hand, there is mind or consciousness, and on the other, matter. Of these two, mind is sentient (that is, it can feel), while matter is non-sentient, or dumb. Because mind is non-material, Descartes said it was outside the realm of scientific enquiry. This set in place a preoccupation for mainstream science with the study of matter, considered to be non-sentient and purposeless. Mind, or consciousness, was left to theology and metaphysics (and more recently, psychology), and was not considered by science to be relevant to understanding reality. This dualism between mind and matter has contributed significantly to the mechanistic, manipulative mindset that underlies the knowledge-based society of today.

Penetrating analyses of the implications of this material bias in science have appeared in books by two authors coming from significantly different backgrounds. Frank Parkinson describes himself as an "unapologetic generalist". His book, *Jehovah and Hyperspace,* explores the interface where science, philosophy and theology meet. Christian de Quincey is a philosopher and professor of consciousness studies at John F. Kennedy University. His book, *Radical Nature: Rediscovering the Soul of Matter* puts forward the thesis that the whole universe, animate and inanimate, is full of consciousness, from the smallest particle to the highest form of human consciousness.

De Quincey is gravely concerned that the Western industrial doctrine of materialism is leading to "inevitable ecological and civilizational collapse."(8) He is critical of both science and religion as failing to provide humanity with a worldview that can sustain us into the future. Science is at fault for it has failed to give us an understanding of the most mysterious phenomenon in the universe—consciousness. Religion is at fault, for it imbues consciousness with an added quality called "soul," and focuses attention away from understanding how to live in the natural world to notions of how to transcend the corruptions of the flesh and prepare ourselves for a world beyond this one. The consequence is an already huge and still growing population fixated on ideas of consumption and manipulation of nature for human gratification.

Parkinson is more hopeful than de Quincey that science and religion can come together to give us a new sustaining worldview. He describes the three revelations of science in the last 150 years that give modern humans not only a different way of looking at the world than anyone whose life ended before the 1930s, but also provide the framework for a new understanding of our spiritual and cosmic origins. The three revelations are Charles Darwin's Theory of Evolution, Max Planck's Theory of the Quantum, and Edwin Hubble's Theory of an Expanding Universe, leading to the conclusion that the universe originated in a singularity called the "Big Bang" some 12-14 billion years ago.(9)

In their criticisms of science and spirituality, de Quincey and Parkinson point the way for a reformation of the knowledge-based society towards a more hopeful future than the one promised by our present knowledge society. We will turn to that in a moment, but first we need to consider the nature of knowledge itself and why it holds such powerful implications for the future.

The Ecology of Knowledge

Over many years, Jerzy Wojciechowski, Professor Emeritus of Philosophy at the University of Ottawa, developed a theory of knowledge, which he calls the "ecology of knowledge." The choice of the term "ecology" to name this theory is instructive, for ecology is essentially a science of relationships. Modern humans not only live in a set of relationships with the natural world, which we had no part in creating, but we also live in a set of relationships with the knowledge we have let loose in the world as an entity in its own right, with an existence of its own and distinct from the knowers who have produced it.

Professor Wojciechowski rightly points out that by and large the accumulation of knowledge in the world is "the logical result of centuries or even millennia of rational, tenacious, well-intentioned efforts of generations of humans laboring, striving to progress so as to liberate themselves from misery, ignorance, fear and subordination to uncontrollable forces. The aim of this striving has been, and still is, the creation of a more satisfactory, more human condition."(10)

That being said, however, the consequence of our pursuit and application of knowledge is that we have become an increasingly powerful means and, at the same time, a growing obstacle to our further development. We have to think about ourselves in terms of the whole species and confront the issue of the survival of the species. "It now becomes evident that, in order to survive, humans have to know and understand themselves more and more and much better than ever before."(11)

Where we are in difficulty, in facing up to this challenge is that modern knowledge, which developed over more than three centuries since Descartes, "is quantitative, factual cognition, which tells us much about how the world is, but little about how we should behave. It is not synonymous with moral progress."(12) Science did not make us morally better, but gave us greater power to do things and thereby to increase our capacity to harm ourselves.

Review

So there we have it: an industrial world awash with knowledge, primarily focused on controlling and manipulating the environment for human advantage; a privileged small proportion of the world's population applying this knowledge to consume the Earth's resources with virtually unrestrained abandon; a few powerful governments and corporations controlling the flow of commerce through a policy of globalization based on continuous growth; a prodigiously powerful assortment of weapons of mass destruction in a number of countries primed and ready for use if their leaders decide to do so; a flood of electronic information carrying the philosophy of growth and consumption to another less industrialized world where the people look enviously at the lifestyles of their more fortunate world citizens and know they can never live like that; another portion of the world's population too poor, sick and malnourished to know anything about what is going on, elsewhere on the planet; a physical environment substantially degraded from its former health; and a mélange of spiritual belief systems rooted in a myth-based past largely irrelevant to the materially minded citizens of the industrialized countries in the 21st century.

That is the darker side of the legacy of the knowledge society to date. Fortunately, there is another brighter side, to which we can turn for inspiration and hope. Let us do so now as we seek to find direction to build bridges to a sustainable future.

FOUNDATIONAL SUPPORTS FOR A MORE ENLIGHTENED KNOWLEDGE SOCIETY

The specter now facing humanity is the extinction rather than the enrichment of life. Therefore, the starting point for reconceptualizing the knowledge society is to identify life-supporting principles for human behavior. These are now available to us from the science of ecology. One part of our task is to make human beings ecoliterate.

Living in Accordance with Ecological Principles

One of the foremost spokesmen for articulating ecological principles is Fritjof Capra, Director of the Center for Ecoliteracy in Berkeley, California. Speaking in 1998 in Prague at a conference of scholars addressing the issue of purposefulness in nature, Capra began with a fundamental question: "How do we need to behave as members of the Earth Household? Well, we need to behave like the other members of the household who, as we have seen, sustain, and even enrich and diversify, the pattern of relationships in the web of life. This is what is meant by ecological sustainability. What needs to be sustained is not competitive advantage, corporate profits, or economic growth. What need to be sustained are the patterns of relationships in the web of life."(13)

Capra went on to outline the basic principles of organization of ecosystems, which should be the model for human organization:

- An ecosystem generates no waste; one species' waste is another species' food.
- Matter cycles continuously through the web of life.
- The energy driving these ecological cycles flows from the sun.
- Diversity assures resilience.
- Life from its beginning progressed by cooperation, partnership and networking.

Capra concluded his remarks with this advice and warning: "The survival of humanity will depend on our ability to understand the principles of ecology, and act and live accordingly. This is an enterprise that transcends all our differences of race, culture or class. The earth is our common home, and creating a sustainable world for our children and for future generations is our common task."

Creating Life-Supporting Economies

Capra asserts that the above ecosystem principles must form the basis of our future technologies, economic systems, and social institutions. "Either that or there will be no future for humanity." Rees picks up the same theme when he argues that our current world economy "exists in a quasi-parasitic relationship with the ecosphere." By maximizing consumption, injecting human waste into the environment, and drawing down non-renewable energy supplies, "the expanding human enterprise is thermodynamically positioned to consume and contaminate—to 'disorder'—the ecosphere from within."(14)

So we must change the fundamental organization of the human enterprise. But change to what and how? Part of the answer was outlined by Hawken, Lovins and Lovins in their ground-breaking 1999 book Natural Capitalism.(15) They outline four central strategies:

- Using resources more effectively
- Mimicking nature to reduce the wasteful throughput of materials
- Creating an economy in which a flow of services rather than acquisition of goods is used to measure progress and affluence
- Investing in sustaining, retaining and exchanging stocks of natural capital.

Another form of capital, Spiritual Capital, also needs to be considered. This is a concept developed by Danah Zohar. She argues that, for capitalism to have a future, it must change its focus from the single-minded accumulation of material capital and begin to accumulate "spiritual capital." She has a vision of capitalism as it could be: a values-based culture in which wealth is accumulated to generate a decent profit while businesses act to raise the common good and ensure the sustainability of their enterprises.(16)

So the strategies and principles for necessary economic change are known. But this knowledge still lies at the margins of the knowledge society. How are they to be brought to center-stage so that the whole nature of our knowledge-based economy begins to change? Obviously, an important part of the answer is to shift our educational systems from support of the flawed knowledge society to creation of something new and different.

Embracing Life-Enhancing Education

Capra speaks of the need for a pedagogy that puts the understanding of life at its very centre so that we overcome the current alienation from the natural world and rekindle a sense of praise and awe for Creation. He also looks for systemic school reform in which the process of learning is based on what we now know of the brain as a complex, highly adaptive, self-organizing system. This means emphasizing experiential learning or project-based learning so that students use the knowledge from various subject areas to engage in complex, real-world projects like creating a school garden or building a model community. Schools would become true learning communities where everyone in the system is both a teacher and a learner.

Complementing academic and practical learning would be the learning of values such as is offered through the Living Values Program.17) This is a UNICEF and UNESCO-sponsored initiative already being offered in over 7000 sites in 74 countries around the world. It is a non-sectarian, multicultural curriculum taught through stories, the natural way that humans learn, emphasizing the importance of living values like respect, cooperation, peace and responsibility.

In Metro Vancouver, the Institute for Ethical Leadership has promoted the Living Values Program to several school jurisdictions and teacher groups in order to introduce this curriculum into public schools. The Institute is also supporting the creation of a nature-based educational initiative known as the Gulf Islands Centre for Ecological Learning to introduce the model of ecoliteracy envisioned by Fritjof Capra.

So the good news is that the models for change exist and efforts are under way all around the world to move them into the mainstream. In higher education, William Rees refers to initiatives where students, faculties and administrative organizations in universities across the developing world are increasingly engaged in special campus projects. He cites the example of the special Sustainability Office at the University of British Columbia and its dedicated Sustainable Development Research Centre and the Graduate School of Community and Regional Planning.

These are examples of what can be done when educators take responsibility for change in the formal educational systems. Small sparks can ignite great fires. An indication that something like that is beginning to take hold in the world can be seen in various international initiatives.

Creating New International Institutions and Forms of Governance to Support Life

As Rees points out, "Creating a socially just and ecologically sustainable global culture...will require new international institutions that can exercise a trans-national veto over certain behavioral dispositions...that are potentially fatal...(the newly established International Criminal Court is a case in point)."(18)

Rees also draws attention to the Earth Charter, another effort supported by UNESCO and other international organizations, which provides an ethical framework to govern relationships on Earth. It includes such principles as:

- Respect Earth and life in all its diversity.
- Care for the community of life with understanding, compassion and love.
- Build democratic societies that are just, participatory, sustainable and peaceful.
- Secure Earth's bounty and beauty for present and future generations.

"These principles recognize that we humans are unlikely to conserve anything for which we do not have love and respect, empathy and compassion. Indeed, it might be argued that for ecological sustainability we must come to feel in our bones that the violation of nature is a violation of self."(19). These same sentiments have been eloquently expressed elsewhere by that great champion of learning from the Book of Nature, Thomas Berry, in *The Great Work*: "The Great Work now, as we move into a new millennium, is to carry out the transition from a period of human devastation of the Earth to a period when humans would be present to the planet in a mutually beneficial manner."(20)

For such a transformation in the human psyche to occur, however, requires rediscovery of what Vaclav Havel has referred to as our "transcendental anchor" and the true purpose of our existence. This goes much deeper than economic or educational reforms. It goes to the core of our understanding of ourselves as spiritual beings and the new story we will tell ourselves of who we are and why we are here.

The New Cosmological Story

Reference was made earlier to the fact that anyone whose life was completed before the 1930s could not have the same worldview as one who lived most of his or her life in the second half of the 20thcentury. The reason is the astonishing revelations by 20th century science on the nature of reality. Arthur Peacocke, physicist and theologian, puts it succinctly: "Science has revealed the deep wonders of the created world to an extent that has altered the whole horizon and context of humanity's thinking about itself."(21)

What is it that science has revealed? Recognizing that all scientific knowledge is a work in progress, proceeding through the development and proposing of theory, through inference to the best explanation, then by testing of the theory through experimentation to tentative acceptance or rejection of the theory—recognizing then that the story may change with new knowledge, this is what modern science says about reality.

The universe emerged as a pinpoint of stupendous energy in an event called the "Big Bang" that was the beginning of what we call time and space. Now, some 12-14 billion years later, we are aware of a vast cosmos of billions of galaxies, still expanding, while here on our tiny planet Earth we know ourselves as human beings who have evolved out of that original cosmic energy.

That is the macro world of cosmology. But we also know of another micro quantum world where matter dissolves into energy and where particles emerge from and disappear into something we call, for want of a better term, the "quantum vacuum." We know of a mysterious quality possessed by ourselves and other creatures called consciousness. We know that our consciousness somehow inexplicably interacts with the quantum world to cause particles to appear from nowhere, to turn a probability into an actuality.

We also know, from the science of complexity and chaos theory, that nature is a highly complex, interlocking network of nested systems, such that it is impossible or difficult to predict accurately the outcome of an intervention. In such a world we cannot control nature because we are part of the system and the most we can do is participate.

On all of the above, most scientists would agree that this is the way it is. However, when we push a little deeper, uncertainties or disavowals appear. But it is into this uncertainty we must push if we are to find any satisfactory answer to Vaclav Havel's question of the true purpose of our existence.

Christian de Quincey argues that what we should understand is that the world is not defined only by its physicality, but that consciousness plays a participatory and determining role. He suggests that consciousness is the quality in the universe that has been able to construct the whole story of the universe. Nature is full of the same mind that we know in ourselves. We are in Nature and Nature is in us.

This leads to the understanding that "Nature is sacred, inherently divine. It is full of God, full of spirit, full of consciousness...The best way to connect with the divinity of Nature is through touching and feeling the Earth and its inhabitants. The way to meaning in our lives is by reconnecting with the world of Nature—through exuberant participation or through the stillness of meditation, just by being present and listening. And when we do so, we hear, we feel, and we learn: we are not alone— we are uniquely special."(22)

If we can do this, says de Quincey, then maybe we can save ourselves from the "otherwise inevitable ecological and civilizational collapse that faces us within our lifetime." In the

Western tradition we have relied too heavily on rational analysis that has taken us into a cul-de-sac of believing and behaving as if everything is separate and in conflict and competition. We have built our national economies, fast becoming the global economy, on this flawed belief, now being refuted by the very science that spawned it.

In a new global civilization, we must learn together how to embrace all ways of knowing (such as exist in non-Western traditions of Taoism, Buddhism, Hinduism, and Shamanism). This is how de Quincey believes we can find our common humanity and our role as conscious participants and co-creators in the great cosmic adventure. But we can go deeper than that to the question of Ultimate Reality and the spiritual significance of our presence on Earth.

A New Spirituality

Both Arthur Peacocke and Frank Parkinson move on from the discoveries of science described above to consider the question of ultimate origin revealed by that science. They are dissatisfied with the explanation by scientists of the stature of Stephen Hawking that the universe merely emerged by accident from an original fluctuating quantum field or "quark soup." Peacocke, the scientist, argues as Peacocke, the theologian, that the best explanation of how the world revealed by science comes to be here in the first place is that it is grounded in what he calls Ultimate Reality. Using the scientific process of inference, Peacocke concludes that this Ultimate Reality can be regarded as a suprapersonal creator God who participates along with his creation in a process of unfolding evolution.

Parkinson argues that the universe emerged as an act of will from a divine source of infinite energy. He is less interested in the notion of a suprapersonal God than in the conviction that because the cosmos emerged as an act of thought from divine consciousness, then everything contained in that absolute consciousness is in the world. This means that all of humanity and everything else in the universe are fundamentally interconnected in spirit.

However, the further extension of this concept that the universe is made up of "God stuff" means that what we know as evolution is "God-in-this-world unfolding." The creating divinity is not separate from what is created. It is the Holy Spirit from which humans are derived as its highest expression of consciousness, which means that we "humans constitute in a unique way this divine spirit in action."(23)

In this explanation, we have found the answer to Vaclav Havel's question. The true purpose of our existence is to be conscious co-creators with the Holy Spirit, who is within us, working with us such that our human spirit is the "Holy Spirit seeking completion in our search for completion."(24)

The unmistakable thrust of this line of thought is one of becoming. It looks forward to the emergence of a new kind of human as different in consciousness from current humanity as we are from our apelike forbears. Parkinson even suggests a name for this new form of *Homo sapiens* as *Homo novus*.

Of course, there is a danger that we may fail to attain this next step in evolution. Vaclav Havel, in his speech in Independence Hall, Philadelphia on July 4, 1994, reminded his audience that: "we are parts of a greater whole. If we endanger her, she will dispense with us in the interest of a higher value—that is, life itself."(25)

Facing this issue, Arthur Peacocke reasons that the only way the on-going process of creation can be achieved is through the evolution of self-conscious, freely choosing beings, namely us. The story of humanity is its struggle to discover and choose life-sustaining values, which by their very nature require free consent of the choosers.

On this subject, three scholars in 1996 spent two intensive days reflecting about the human condition and the possible future. Sociologist Ervin Laszlo, psychologist Stan Graf and physicist, Peter Russell, came to the conclusion that consciousness was the key issue above everything else. Their reflections have been published in a book called *The Consciousness Revolution*. An excerpt appeared in the Spring 2004 issue of *Living Lightly*.

Laszlo puts it this way: "Perhaps it is not entirely exaggerated to say that there is such a thing as a mind of humanity, something like a noosphere, a collective unconscious operating in and around all of us, which is now beginning to show up in the consciousness of individuals."(26). Graf pointed to the sudden and unexpected collapse of the Soviet Union as an example of this shift in consciousness in action. Russell concluded that "changing consciousness is valuable in itself. Maybe it will lead to a world in which we can avoid some of the catastrophes. Maybe it will not. But either way it is absolutely essential." (27)

For another perspective on how well we are doing on the quest for changing consciousness and life-sustaining values, we can turn to historical analysis, culminating in the achievement of the Universal Declaration of Human Rights on December 10, 1948.

From Ancient Traditions to Human Rights

An engrossing account of human progress from ancient times to the 20th century has been provided by Charlotte Waterlow in *The Hinge of History*. She argues that history shows that in traditional societies preceding civilization there was no clear understanding of the significance of personhood. Culture was collective, set within the context of a universe which was regarded as divine. In the modern age a supreme leap forward is being taken into the understanding and expression of personhood, but there is great confusion about its divine context.(28)

In other words, we have made great progress in articulating the idea that a world society can be built upon the foundations of a moral code as set forth in the Universal Declaration of Human Rights, but we have lost touch with the Source of those Rights. Our secular society is proceeding on the assumption that we can change the world as we like by using and applying the knowledge given to us by science, and we are making a mess of it.

Again the voice of Vaclav Havel can be heard on this issue, in the same speech quoted above. If the idea of human rights "is to be more than just a slogan mocked by half the world," it must be anchored in a different place, in the understanding that we are mysteriously connected to the entire universe. "Only someone who submits to the authority of the universal order and of Creation, who values the right to be a part of it and participate in it, can genuinely value himself and his neighbors and thus honor their rights as well."(29) In these last statements we are coming to the nub of the issue for future human progress.

Charlotte Waterlow argues that, having achieved the sense of personhood, the way forward is through "the doctrine that the universe is full of persons, united by love." This is the only way we can find a solution to our central human problem of envisioning the goals for the evolution of our planet. Notably, this is also the doctrine of "the warm heart" proclaimed by the Dalai Lama. His message consistently repeated as he travels throughout the world is that "true happiness comes not from a limited concern for one's own well-being, or that of those one feels close to, but from developing love and compassion for all sentient beings."(30). The Dalai Lama sees the cultivation of these human qualities as part of the educational process. Significantly, in April 2004, he was in Vancouver to participate in a round table conference on this subject with other visionary leaders addressing the topic "Balancing Educating the Mind with Educating the Heart." Is the modern secular world of corporate profits, economic globalization, nuclear power, and missile defense systems ready to listen to the doctrine of the warm heart and universal love?

CONCLUSION

We began this inquiry into the nature and viability of the knowledge society with a question from Vaclav Havel. Does our reluctance or inability to address the major issues confronting humanity, despite our already vast and increasing knowledge, not imply that something needs to change in "the sphere of the spirit?" Do we not need to understand differently and more perfectly "the true purpose of our existence?"

We examined the issue from the perspective of several disciplines and lines of enquiry: ecological economics (William Rees); systems thinking (Donella Meadows); cosmology and theology (Frank Parkinson and Arthur Peacocke); philosophy of consciousness (Christian de Quincey); ecology and education (Fritjof Capra); ecology and economics (Paul Hawken, Amory Lovins and L. Hunter Lovins); spiritual economics (Danah Zohar); philosophy of knowledge (Jerzy Wojciechowski); values-based education (Living Values Program); global sustainability (the Earth Charter); history of cultures (Thomas Berry); sociology, psychology and physics (Ervin Laszlo, Stan Graf and Peter Russell); history of civilizations (Charlotte Waterlow); and Buddhist spirituality (the Dalai Lama).

If our transdisciplinary enquiry has been helpful it should have created new intellectual space, generated emergent knowledge, and enlarged our future choices. It should have opened up our minds (and hearts) to new possibilities and warned us of the dangers of unwise choices. What, indeed, have we learned from this enquiry?

We have learned that the dominant economic policy of the industrialized world manifesting in a process of economic globalization is, in fact, unquestioning acceptance of the cultural myth of sustainability through growth, which positions an ever expanding human enterprise to increasingly consume and contaminate the ecosphere on which we depend for life. The science and technology from which this enterprise is derived places unconditional faith in objective reality but fails to connect with the human need for intrinsic meaning. The knowledge derived from this science base tells us much about how the world works, but does little for moral improvement. We achieve greater power to do but make little progress on how to be.

Though the cumulative thrust of this knowledge-based enterprise is essentially destructive, it nevertheless carries within it the seeds of a new genesis. The science of ecology reveals the principles on which nature has maintained conditions of sustainability over hundreds of millions of years. A new pedagogy of ecoliteracy can guide human creativity to embrace these ecological principles in the design of human organizations and institutions. Initiatives such as the Earth Charter and the Living Values Program, though still at the margins of human activity, are growing in influence and hold great potential for making qualitative improvement.

However, if we are to reach down deep to effect change in what Vaclav Havel calls "the sphere of the spirit," we must search within the dominant knowledge system of science for transcendent ideas. These are now emerging in the nexus between science and religion, where revelations of science provide an understanding of human evolution as an expression of divine intent. The true purpose of our existence is seen as a continuous process of co-creation with the Original Consciousness or Ultimate Reality, from which the living universe is derived. Evidence of human progress in this direction is seen in the Universal Declaration of Human Rights, but we must now embrace multiple ways of knowing that will transcend our current preoccupation with self-interest to release our human potential for love and compassion for all of Creation.

We stand at the threshold of this new genesis. There is a sense of shift in the human ethos "as if something is on the way out and something else is painfully being born."(31) This has happened before in human history but never on the scale of a global civilization and never when the stakes have been as high as the extinction of the species.

This is the challenge we face in creating a knowledge society sufficiently robust and enlightened to sustain the human enterprise within the ecosphere from which we are derived. Let us accept the challenge with goodwill, strong hearts and unlimited courage and determination to succeed.

REFERENCES

1. Vaclav Havel, Forum 2000, September 4, 1997
2. William Rees, "Globalization and Sustainability: Conflict or Consequence," *Bulletin of Science, Technology and Society*, August 2002
3. William Rees, op. cit.
4. William Rees, "Impeding Sustainability? The Ecological Footprint of Higher Education," *Planning for Higher Education*, March-May 2003
5. William Rees, op. cit.
6. Donella Meadows, "Dancing with Systems," *Timeline*, March-April 2004
7. Donella Meadows, op. cit.
8. Christian de Quincey, *Radical Nature: Rediscovering the Soul of Matter*, (Vermont: Invisible Cities Press, 2002)
9. Frank Parkinson, *Jehovah and Hyperspace: Exploring the Future of Science, Religion and Society* (London: New European Publications, 2002)
10. Jerzy A. Wojceichowski, *Ecology of Knowledge* (Washington: The Council for Research in Values and Philosophy, 2001)
11. Jerzy A. Wojceichowski, op. cit
12. Jerzy A. Wojceichowski, op. cit.
13. Fritjof Capra, "Is There a Purpose in Nature?" *Forum 2000*, March 22-25, 1998
14. William Rees, "Globalization and Sustainability: Conflict or Consequence," *Bulletin of Science, Technology and Society*, August 2002
15. Paul Hawken, Amory Lovins, L. Hunter Lovins, *Natural Capitalism* (New York: Little, Brown and Company, 1999)
16. Danah Zohar, Spiritual Capitalism: Wealth We can Live By (Berrett-Kochler, 2004)
17. *Living Values: An Educational Program* (Deerfield Beach, Florida: Health Communications, Inc. 2000)
18. William Rees, "Impeding Sustainability? The Ecological Footprint of Higher Education," *Planning for Higher Education*, March-May 2003

19. William Rees, "Globalization and Sustainability: Conflict or Consequence," *Bulletin of Science, Technology and Society,* August 2002
20. Thomas Berry, *The Great Work: Our Way into the Future* (New York: Bell Tower, 1999)
21. Arthur Peacocke, *Paths from Science Towards God* (Oxford: One World Publications, 2001)
22. Christian de Quincey, op. cit.
23. Frank Parkinson, op. cit.
24. Frank Parkinson, op. cit.
25. Vaclav Havel, "The Need for Transcendence in the Postmodern World," Speech delivered in Independence Hall, Philadelphia, July 4, 1994.
26. "The Consciousness Revolution" *Living Lightly,* Spring 2004
27. "The Consciousness Revolution" op. cit.
28. Charlotte Waterlow, *The Hinge of History* (London: The One World Trust, 1995)
29. Vaclav Havel, op. cit.
30. The Dalai Lama, precise reference unknown
31. Vaclav Havel, op. cit.

A New Balance:
Giving Attention to the Feminine Voice

The material world pulses with the rhythm of a universe connected in a manner so complex and intricate and at a level so small that the microscope needed to see it has not yet been invented. The science through which we understand reality is at the cusp of such a transformation of knowing that all of our previous experience with such moments of change has not prepared the way. A trillion trillion threads at the quantum level are weaving themselves into new patterns of life, learning continuously how to be better adapted to the future ahead.

Decades away from this moment the pattern and the fabric of life will be so different we would not recognize it from our present vantage point. Like the growth of a child in our family, we cannot see the pattern changing because our daily observations are not able to detect the minute changes taking place in front of us, simple act by simple act, incident by incident.

Life adapts in order to continue. Great threats to our survival as a species affected all life in the 20th century. We saw them writ large on September 11, 2001 as the consciousness driven by hatred and bent on destruction had its way. While others might focus on the damaging effects of human activity on the environment and on the biosphere, I will raise my voice here to focus more deeply on what I see as the ultimate causal factors of the dangers of our time.

Fear and Attachment

Two primordial emotions govern all life: fear and attachment. To the degree that fear governs society we have seen war and suffering playing out the human drama of the last 10,000 years. The reason is that the way to overcome fear is to take control: to be bigger, stronger, faster, more cruel, more punishing and thus win the moment for yourself, your tribe, your nation. At the deepest levels of the consciousness that connects us, the pain and suffering along with the building of our current civilizations have been spurred by this fear.

But yet, if the only emotion receiving expression were fear, we would not have survived. Pulsing with the life force, and more powerful than fear, is the binding power of attachment that begins when a mother cares for her young. Through the emotion of this attachment we learn a different truth than that of fear, and through this learning we create and nurture our common future.

It is the force of attachment that allows us to evolve our intelligence. While today's reality seems overcome by fear, there are a million trends that cumulatively can bring us to a bifurcation point where the balance tips away from fear towards attachment and nurture. The message then is to use our intelligence to view life and reality with the lens that searches out, reveals and highlights acts of goodness. These are the experiences that enhance life and give us the wisdom to understand the destructiveness of fear and to see fear mongering for what it is.

Raising the Voices of Women

Because the stakes are now so high and because the danger of the degradation of all life is so real, the importance of speaking out becomes essential for a new way of living together on this fragile planet. Feminine intelligence, genetically programmed for nurture and attachment, now needs to prevail, not by seeking to overcome but rather to redress the balance and bring the masculine intelligence to also see its nurturing side.

Can you imagine an Afghanistan where women are equally respected and as powerful as men? How different would it be from the country of today where the harboring of terror and the perpetration of fear have wreaked their devastation? Can you imagine a future for Afghanistan where mothers and daughters, educated along with fathers and sons, take an equal place in parliament and in the institutions and places of business and commerce and in the very life of the country?

Can you imagine an America, a Britain or a Russia where the mothers have equal voice?

Riane Eisler in her book, *The Chalice and the Blade*, tells of a time in history where the feminine voice was honored and heard. In her book, *The Power of Partnership*, she provides hundreds of examples of how the reality of true partnering between men and women enhance every aspect of business and industry. In *Tomorrow's Children* she proposes that caring for life for the self, for others and for our Mother Earth should be a thread running through the educational curriculum from preschool to graduate school. It should be an integral part of every child's education. Can you imagine the communities of citizens who were educated in this way?

We need to foster the conditions that encourage caring relationships, and we can do this by building cultures worldwide that value the voices of women as equal partners.

Bringing Dignity to Global Life

We should examine how we are supporting without question through aid, trade and tourism countries that are denigrating half of their population through suppression. No wonder these societies are in a perpetual state of rage, anger and fear that we see acted out on our television screens. Deprived of the dignity caring and nurture could create in *this* life even regardless of economic prosperity, they see themselves as better off dead so they can reap the reward of life after death. A people infused with such beliefs cannot possibly create the conditions that would make this life worth living.

There is a great need for a new global value system that honors the need of life, all life, for care, nurture and attachment. There is a great need for honesty with regard to the short-term gain that comes from agreeing to perpetuate lesser values in countries that are not prepared to come up to this standard.

Wherever societies have respected our humanity and allowed a voice to women as well as men, those communities have flourished. It is the one principle across cultures that stands out in history as a universal good.

Restoring the Balance

Today in the Western world a million trends are pushing in the direction of a new balance, a new human partnership. In institutions of higher learning classes of lawyers, doctors and scientists are now half filled with women. Boardrooms of institutions of big business are moving to include the feminine voice, and small businesses everywhere are benefiting from the energy and enterprise of women. Attention is now given to the wisdom and thoughtfulness of women elders. Wherever this is happening there is a benefit to the human commons.

Last Words: Reaching for Higher Ground

In the global village in which educated men and women now live their lives, the time has come to recognize some essential universal truths that cross every border and boundary we have created in the past. At our core, in every culture and country we are overwhelmingly alike. We are governed by the two primordial emotions of fear and attachment. The feminine instinct is to follow attachment. To the degree that a society, a culture, a community, or even a business allows expression of the human drive to love and to nurture, that arena has been and will be filled with peace, the necessary underpinning for prosperity, health and well-being.

In our time the lessons of history show that where fear, war mongering, and greed have prevailed the spoils of victory are temporary. Voices preaching peace, love, justice and fair play, whether religious or secular, last across the centuries.

It is time that the sons and daughters of every human culture pay heed to their mothers' injunctions for care, compassion and nurture. If the generations of leaders now in charge of the world allow this expression of our common human nobility, what a legacy we will leave.

APPENDIX

Using the Scales for Applied Research

Applied Research

Evidence-Based Outcomes and the Scientific Method

The Ethical Leadership Scales may be used as part of an applied research intervention to measure changes in ethical competence based on this intervention.

To do this the intervention procedures must be set up in advance.

1. To advance knowledge in science a hypothesis is generated that proposes what the intervention is likely to do.

2. The baseline is then established so that the change created by the intervention can be measured. This is done using any or all of the Scales as a *pretest* before the training or intervention begins. In this case the first administration of the Scales should take place without discussion as a moment of quiet reflection in the first hour of the program.

3. **The intervention is then applied.** The procedures and processes are described in detail so that they may be replicated (repeated).

4. The intervention is then followed by a *post test*. In this case the Scales are administered again.

5. Statistical measures are then used to determine whether the effect was significant as a whole or in part, or not significant – that is, due to chance. If the data show that the intervention made a measurable significant difference, the particular intervention, described in detail, is ready to be replicated. These results are published, preferably in peer reviewed journals, or if these are not available, in monograph form, or both, so that others in the field can benefit from the information. When there has been sufficient replication, the intervention is added to the knowledge bank of humanity. It can then be used with greater certainty that the desired outcome will be achieved.

6. In the use of the Ethical Leadership Scales, participants will enter the *pretest* with a particular style of personal judgment. Some will give themselves universally high scores. Others will give themselves low or average scores. In a research situation, where the particular testee is unknown (anonymous) the scores themselves are not as relevant as the change in the scores. After training low scorers may rate themselves higher and high scorers may give themselves more realistic appraisals. The effectiveness of the training may be measured by a

change in the scores. Analysis of Variance procedures that measure these changes will allow the researchers to determine the effectiveness of the training under consideration.

Some Practical Suggestions

As the discipline, practice and training for ethical leadership expands, it would be very useful to integrate the Ethical Leadership Scales into the programs themselves.

Where a university chooses to include education for ethical competence in its training programs in leadership, or where a business organization chooses to improve the ethical competence of its leaders and other personnel, the Ethical Leadership Scales can serve both as a measure of the effectiveness of the training or courses and as a basis for discussion of the ethical issues at the time of the intervention. This process will add rigor and definition to the procedures undertaken. In this way, the Scales may stand alone as a teaching tool.

Since the characteristics described in the Scales are universal across cultures, the Scales are available for translation with discussion and permission from the authors. It should be noted, however, that the administration of the Scales and the dialogue and discussion based on them are meant to be facilitated by leaders trained in their use.

Research Forms

Included at the end of this Appendix is an example of the Research Form for each Scale.

To protect the anonymity of the participants each person is given a randomly generated research number, which is recorded in both the *pretest* and *post test* at the top of the form, or in an appropriate way in an online format. This number will be used to compare pre and post test data. It can also be used to inform anonymously the participants or groups of participants whether there was a significant difference in their pre and post test scores.

The research number can also be used for a third administration at a later time (say, 6 months) to determine whether there has been a lasting or sustained effect following the training or intervention.

To fill out the Research Form testees merely record the values from their Personal Record Forms onto the Research Form and return it to the researcher in a covering envelope. In an online format this can be done in private in a secure way.

As a further benefit researchers may look at individual items or clusters of items to determine the effect of their intervention on particular factors. This procedure can help evaluate aspects of their courses or programs that need to be improved. Repeated use of the Scales can *determine if the changes have been effective.*

The authors of these Scales are researchers and would be very interested in collaborating with other researchers who are interested in using the Scales either as an educational tool or as a research instrument. To explore this possibility, please contact the authors through the website www.ethicalleadership.com.

Research Form
Ethical Competence Scale

Personal Ethical Competence

    Foundational Characteristics   **Value Chosen**

1.	Trustworthiness	_____
2.	Conscientiousness	_____
3.	Consistency	_____
4.	Steadfastness	_____
5.	Integrity	_____
6.	Transparency	_____

    Action Characteristics

7.	Learning Oriented	_____
8.	Courage	_____
9.	Determination	_____
10.	Optimism	_____
11.	Initiative	_____
12.	Thoroughness	_____

Social Ethical Competence

    Empathy

13.	Understanding Others	_____
14.	Respecting Others	_____
15.	Caring About Others	_____
16.	Developing Others	_____
17.	Serving Others	_____

    Social Skills

18.	Communication	_____
19.	Conflict Management	_____
20.	Inspiration	_____
21.	Building Bonds	_____
22.	Cooperation	_____
23.	Collaboration	_____
24.	Team Effort	_____

Global Ethical Competence

    Connections

25.	Interdependence	_____
26.	Stewardship	_____
27.	Global Citizenship	_____

    Future Orientation

28.	Future Orientation	_____
29.	Strategic Visioning	_____
30.	Action Planning	_____

                                                   TOTAL_____

Divide by 3 = EthQ   _____

Research Form
Ethical Leadership Scale

Relationship to Self	Value Chosen	Relationship to Others	Value Chosen
1. Acts with Integrity	_____	26. Compassionate	_____
2. Trustworthy	_____	27. Fair	_____
3. Authentic	_____	28. Democratic	_____
4. Humble	_____	29. Focused on Service	_____
5. Intuitive	_____	30. Focused on Relationships	_____
6. Visionary	_____	31. Believes in the Worth	
7. Hopeful	_____	of Others	_____
8. Creative	_____	32. Synergistic	_____
9. Patient	_____	33. Encourages Teamwork	_____
10. Confident	_____	34. Acts As a Model and	
11. Clear Communicator	_____	Motivator of Others	_____
12. Learning Oriented	_____	35. Nurtures Others	_____
13. Open-Minded	_____	36. Believes in Human Dignity	_____
14. Thinks Clearly	_____		
15. Knowledgeable	_____	**Relationship to the Whole**	
16. Flexible	_____	37. Focused on Reality	_____
17. Attuned	_____	38. Tolerates Contradiction	
18. Proactive	_____	and Anxiety	_____
19. Displays Positive Energy	_____	39. Systems Thinker	_____
20. Adventurous	_____	40. Ecologically Conscious	_____
21. Courageous	_____		
22. Has high Self-Esteem	_____		
23. Focused on Meaning	_____		
24. Believes in Greatness	_____		
25. Holds a Sense of Destiny	_____		

TOTAL _____

Divide by 4 = EthLQ _____

Research Form
Ethical Organization Scale

Factor		Value Chosen
1.	Economic Considerations	_____
2.	Relationship with the workforce	_____
3.	Relationships with contractors and suppliers	_____
4.	Relationships with customers or clients	_____
5.	Relationships with the community	_____
7.	Relationships with the State/Province, Country and the World	_____
7.	Ecological relationships	_____
8.	Cultural relationships	_____
9.	Social responsibility	_____
10.	Holistic perspective	_____

TOTAL _____

EthOQ _____

Printed in the United States
By Bookmasters